# CAKES & BISCUITS

### MARY NORWAK

WARD LOCK LIMITED · LONDON

D1494707

First published in Great Britain in 1985
by Ward Lock Limited, 82 Gower Street,
London WC1E 6EQ an Egmont Company.

Text filmset in Linotron Goudy Old Style
by HBM Typesetting, Chorley, Lancs.
Printed and bound in Italy by Sagdos SpA.

**British Library Cataloguing in Publication Data**

Norwak, Mary
    Cakes and biscuits. (Ward Lock's cookery series)
    1. Cake
    I. Title
    641.8'653    TX771

ISBN 0-7063-6381-7

# Contents

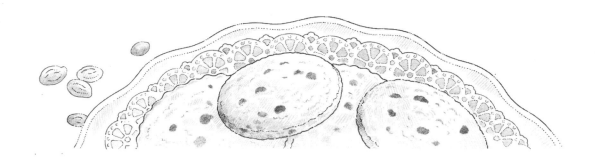

## Acknowledgements

Cover photograph and photography on pages 13, 21, 29, 37, 41, 61, 65 **and** 77 by Annie Morris
Home Economist   Jackie Baxter
Stylist   Sue Brown

Illustrations by Paul Saunders

Equipment for photography kindly loaned by Covent Garden Kitchen Supplies, David Mellor **and** Tea Time.

The author and publisher would like to thank Fyffes Group Ltd for sponsoring the photograph on page 21
**and**
The California Raisin Advisory Board (page 25), Tate and Lyle Refineries (pages 49 and 57), and The Milk Marketing Board (page 53) for supplying photographs.

## Notes

It is important to follow the metric, imperial or American measures when using the recipes in this book. Do not use a combination of measures.

American terminology within recipes is indicated by the use of brackets in both the list of ingredients and in the methods.

American measures which follow metric and imperial measures within the recipe methods are preceded by the term 'US'.

All sugar is granulated, unless otherwise stated.

# INTRODUCTION TO CAKEMAKING

Cakemaking is one of the most enjoyable and absorbing branches of cookery, but must be undertaken with considerable care. It is vital to follow recipes exactly, measuring ingredients meticulously, mixing in the specified way, using the correct size and shape of container, selecting the specified temperature, and timing baking exactly. Follow these basic rules and you will have success after success.

## Equipment

### MIXING

Cakes may be successfully made with no more than a mixing bowl and a wooden spoon. A rotary or wire whisk, hand-held electric beater, electric mixer or food processor will speed up the mixing process considerably, but do remember that it is very important that cakes should not be overbeaten since this will toughen the texture. Another basic piece of kitchen equipment useful in some kinds of cakemaking is a heavy-based saucepan for melting ingredients such as fat or syrup without risk of burning.

### CAKE TINS (PANS)

To ensure perfect results, it is essential to use the exact type of tin (pan) specified in a recipe. Cake tins (pans) come in a great variety of shapes and sizes, and if you enjoy cakemaking, you will probably build up quite a collection. For sponge cakes, 17.5cm/7 inch or 20cm/8 inch shallow round tins (pans), often called 'sandwich' tins (layer pans) are most commonly used in pairs. For layered gâteaux, 22.5cm/9 inch shallow round tins (pans) are most suitable. Deeper tins (pans) are required for fruit cakes and plain cakes: 17.5cm/7 inch or 20cm/8 inch is the most useful size. Loose-bottomed or springform tins (pans) enable cakes to be removed easily. Square and rectangular tins (pans), about 3.75–5cm/1½–2 inches deep, are ideal for tray-baked cakes and gingerbreads. Shallower rectangular Swiss roll tins (jelly roll pans) (the most common size is 32.5 × 22.5cm/13 × 9 inches) may also be used for flapjacks and biscuit mixtures to be cut into squares or fingers. Loaf tins (pans) and bun trays are always useful, while ovenproof ring cake moulds, plain or fluted, are available for savarins, gugelhupf, etc.

Greaseproof paper or non-stick silicone paper is essential when lining tins (pans) and baking sheets. Rice paper is required for a few special cakes such as macaroons, and small paper cases (baking cups) are useful for individual cakes, especially for children's parties.

**Lining a cake tin (pan)**

1 Cut two pieces of greaseproof or non-stick silicone paper to fit the base of the tin (pan).
2 Cut a strip of greaseproof paper 5cm/2 inches wider than the depth of the tin (pan) and long enough to go right round the sides and overlap by 2.5cm/1 inch.
3 Make a 2.5cm/1 inch fold all along the length of the strip. Cut snips at right angles to the edge at 1.25cm/½ inch intervals just to reach the fold.
4 Grease the cake tin (pan), place one of the paper bases in the bottom and grease again.
5 Fit the strip inside the cake tin (pan) with the folded cut edge on the bottom. Press in well. Grease the lining paper.
6 Grease the remaining paper base, and place in the bottom of the tin (pan), greased side up. (For lighter cake mixtures, the second paper base may be omitted. In this case, line the tin (pan) with the strip first, then place the paper base in the bottom.)

# Ingredients

## FLOUR

Flour should be plain (all purpose) when specified, and is essential for cake mixtures which require little raising agent. Self-raising (self-rising) flour is used in lighter cakes. Wholemeal (wholewheat) flour and 81% extraction flour, available in both plain (all purpose) and self-raising (self-rising) types, are particularly suitable for farmhouse-style cakes, but may be substituted for white flour in most recipes except light sponges: a little extra liquid may be needed, as wholemeal (wholewheat) flour is more absorbent than white.

## RAISING AGENTS

These are used in some cake mixtures to give an extra light texture. Baking powder reacts with moisture to form a gas which makes small bubbles: these expand quickly and are set by heat to give an airy lightness to the finished cake. Bicarbonate of soda (baking soda) is often used with honey or treacle (molasses) to neutralize acids and give a soft texture, as in gingerbread. Yeast is used as the raising agent in some rich cakes such as babas, savarins and gugelhupf.

## SWEETENING AGENTS

These may be widely varied and used to give different results in terms of flavour and texture. Caster (fine) sugar dissolves quickly in whisked and creamed mixtures, and is, therefore, best in sponge cakes. Granulated sugar is suitable for many plain and fruit cakes. Soft brown sugar, either light or dark, gives a rich flavour and colour: dark brown sugar is good for gingerbreads, other spice cakes and rich fruit cakes, and light brown sugar for light fruit cakes. Demerara (brown) sugar, being grainy in texture, is usually reserved for flapjacks and cake toppings.

Golden (light corn) syrup is sweet, light and bland, while black treacle (molasses) gives a distinctive flavour, texture and colour to baking. Honey is delicious in many cakes. When using it as a substitute for sugar, replace only one-third of the sugar total by honey, or the cake will over brown during baking. Dried and candied fruit, including apricots, dates, cherries and cut peel, contain plenty of natural sweetness, but should not be substituted for other sweetening agents since they will affect the texture of the cake.

## EGGS

Eggs give volume, colour and flavour to cakes. They should be used at room temperature, not straight from a refrigerator. They must be carefully separated, if this is specified, so that no yolk is left in the white, since the fat from the yolk will lessen the volume of the whisked whites.

## DRIED FRUIT

Dried fruit should be plump, fresh and clean: discard any pips or stems before use. A large piece of candied peel cut to taste will have a stronger, fresher flavour than ready-bought cut mixed peel. Dates are best bought in a block and chopped, although ready-chopped sugar-rolled dates are also available. Glacé (candied) cherries are heavy with syrup and need to be thoroughly washed and dried before use to prevent them sinking to the bottom during baking.

# Methods

## RUBBING-IN

This is used for plain cakes and some biscuits (cookies). The fat is rubbed into the flour with the fingertips, as in pastry-making, so that the mixture does not become sticky. Rubbing-in should be done very lightly, and the mixture lifted as much as possible to incorporate maximum air. The finished rubbed-in mixture should resemble fine breadcrumbs.

## CREAMING

This is the most frequently used method in cakemaking, and is used for richer cakes. The fat should be at room temperature but not oily, and should be creamed with sugar either with a wooden spoon or a mixer or food processor at medium speed, until the texture is light and fluffy and the mixture is pale in colour.

## WHISKING

This method is used for very light cakes such as fatless sponges: the air is incorporated by whisking together whole eggs and sugar, or egg whites and sugar, until the mixture is very light and fluffy. When whole eggs are used, the mixture will resemble whipped cream. If egg whites only are used, the mixture will form soft peaks, then stiff peaks. Generally, the 'soft peak' stage is the one to aim for in cakemaking, but 'stiff peaks' are essential for meringue-making. With either whisked or creamed mixtures, folding-in should be done as lightly as possible, with a large metal spoon, using a figure-of-eight motion to lift the heavier substance from the bottom of the bowl. Lighter mixtures should always be folded into heavier ones.

## MELTING

This is the method used for making gingerbread and some moist fruit cakes. The fat, sugar and syrup are heated gently until the fat has melted before being mixed with the dry ingredients.

## BEATING

Beating follows the melting or creaming of ingredients which are then incorporated into dry ingredients. Some cakes such as gingerbreads need vigorous beating with a wooden spoon, electric mixer or food processor, but overbeating will spoil any cake. The consistency of the beaten mixture is important to ensure the correct texture in the finished cake. A *soft dropping* consistency means that the mixture should drop easily from a spoon without being shaken, but is too stiff to pour. A *stiff dropping* consistency means the mixture will keep its shape when shaken from a spoon, but is too soft and sticky to handle.

## BAKING AND COOLING

The correct oven temperature is crucial to successful cakemaking. Rich fruit cakes and cakes containing syrup (such as gingerbread) are generally baked at a low-to-moderate temperature, lighter cakes at moderate-to-high. It is important not to open the oven door during baking, or the cake will sink: a glass oven door is very helpful here.

When correctly baked, a cake should be well-risen, golden, firm and springy when pressed lightly. Cakes will shrink slightly from the edges of the tin, and a very thin skewer inserted into the centre of the cake should come out clean.

After removal from the oven, a cake should be left in its tin (pan) for a minute or two to firm up sufficiently before being turned out. Rich fruit cakes can be left to cool for up to an hour in the tin (pan), until just warm, while tray-baked cakes may be cooled and iced in the tin (pan). Cooling should be completed on a wire cake rack, and cakes must be completely cold before being stored in a tin or polythene container, or before being frozen (see page 10).

# Common Faults and their Causes

## BADLY CRACKED ON TOP OR 'PEAKED'

Too much raising agent. Too much mixture in tin (pan). Too much or too little liquid. Oven too hot or cake too near top of oven.

## TOP SUNK IN MIDDLE

Too much raising agent. Too much liquid. Baking tin (pan) too small for mixture. Not baked long enough. Oven too cool. Slamming oven door during baking.

## TUNNELLING IN CENTRE OF CAKE

Over mixing when adding flour. Mixture too dry, causing air pockets. Insufficient blending of raising agent and flour.

## FRUIT SUNK TO BOTTOM

Mixture too set. Fruit too wet. Glacé (candied) fruit too syrupy. Fruit too large and heavy. Oven too low.

## SPECKLING ON TOP OF CAKE

Insufficient blending of raising agent and flour. Too much sugar. Sugar too coarse. Insufficient creaming.

## YELLOW SPOTS IN CAKE

Too much bicarbonate of soda (baking soda). Soda not well dissolved in liquid. Dry ingredients not sufficiently sifted.

## TEXTURE TOO COARSE

Fat and sugar insufficiently creamed or fat not well rubbed into flour, or eggs and sugar insufficiently whisked. Inadequate final beating. Too much raising agent. Oven too low.

## RUBBERY TEXTURE

Overmixing. Too much egg and/or milk. Dry, crumbly texture. Too little liquid. Fat not rubbed in sufficiently. Too much raising agent. Baking too slow.

## UNEVEN TEXTURE

Fat not well rubbed in. Insufficient mixing. Air pockets caused by not putting mixture into tin (pan) all at once.

# Freezing

Many cakes, plain or rich, freeze well, and, if you have a large freezer, you may find that a 'batch bake' from time to time proves an excellent money- and time-saver. Sponge cakes which do not keep long after baking, are particularly well worth freezing. Rich fruit cakes, however, which keep so well in a tin or other sealed container need not be frozen.

Cakes may be frozen undecorated or decorated, and raw cake mixtures may also be frozen. Sandwich (layer) cakes filled with buttercream will freeze satisfactorily, but fruit and jam fillings should be avoided as these will make the cake soggy.

## UNDECORATED CAKES

Wrap in foil, or seal in freezer-proof polythene bags. Very large cakes may be packaged in rigid cake containers, or cut into slices for individual packaging and easy thawing. Package sandwich (layer) cakes with a disc of waxed paper between the layers. Swiss rolls (jelly rolls) to be frozen unfilled should be rolled up in cornflour (cornstarch) rather than sugar. Small undecorated cakes may be packaged together in usable quantities in polythene bags. Freeze undecorated cakes for up to 4 months, yeast-raised cakes for up to 3 months.

Thaw in packaging at room temperature, allowing 1 hour for small cakes, 1½–2 hours for sponge cakes, 2–2½ hours for Swiss rolls (jelly rolls), 2–3 hours for larger cakes.

## DECORATED CAKES

Buttercream, almond paste and fresh whipped cream freeze well, but fondant, glacé and royal icings and boiled icings such as American frosting do not freeze. Open-freeze decorated cakes to avoid damage to decoration, then wrap in foil or polythene and place in a rigid container. Freeze for up to 3 months.

Remove the wrapping before thawing to prevent the wrapping sticking to the decoration, then thaw as for undecorated cakes. Cakes containing fresh dairy cream are best sliced while still partially frozen.

## RAW CAKE MIXTURES

Rich creamed mixtures freeze satisfactorily, but whisked sponges should be avoided.

Freeze the mixture in sealed polythene containers or cartons, or fill a cake tin (pan) lined with greased foil, then open-freeze, remove and seal in foil. Freeze for up to 2 months.

Thaw the mixture in its container at room temperature for 2–3 hours, then bake. Return the mixture frozen in a tin (pan) shape to the original tin and bake from frozen in a pre-heated oven for 5 minutes longer than the specified baking time for a sandwich cake, and 10–15 minutes longer for deeper cakes.

## RAW BISCUIT (COOKIE) MIXTURES

Any biscuit (cookie) mixture containing over 100g/4 oz/8 US tablespoons fat to 450g/1 lb/4 US cups flour freezes satisfactorily.

Biscuit (cookie) mixtures for cutting out should be frozen in rolls of the same diameter as the required biscuit (cookie). Soft mixtures can be piped before freezing.

To freeze, wrap each roll in foil, and seal. Pipe or spoon soft biscuit (cookie) mixtures on to a baking sheet, and open-freeze. Lift off with a palette knife (metal spatula), and pack in polythene bags or containers. Freeze for up to 6 months.

To thaw, leave rolls of mixture in their foil at room temperature until soft enough to slice. Bake as normal. Place frozen piped or spooned mixtures on a baking sheet, and bake at the normal temperature, allowing about 5 minutes longer than the specified time.

# FAMILY CAKES

In this chapter you will find a wide selection of cakes suitable for everyday. All are easy to make, store well, and for this reason, as well as for their popularity, they are sometimes described as 'cut and come again'.

Before beginning any of the recipes, look through the Introduction to cakemaking methods on pages 7–10. Be sure to assemble all the ingredients and weigh them out before you start to make the cake. Do not forget to pre-heat the oven. Grease the tin (pan) and line it if necessary (see page 7) before you begin to prepare the mixture, so that it can be turned straight into the tin (pan) and baked immediately without loss of the air which will give the cake its lightness.

## COCONUT CAKE

| Metric/imperial | | American |
|---|---|---|
| 225g/8 oz | plain (all purpose) flour | 2 cups |
| 2 × 5ml spoons/ 2 teaspoons | baking powder | 3 teaspoons |
| | a pinch of salt | |
| 75g/3 oz | butter **or** margarine, diced | 6 tablespoons |
| 75g/3 oz | sugar | scant $\frac{1}{2}$ cup |
| 50g/2 oz | desiccated (shredded) coconut | $\frac{3}{4}$ cup, loosely packed |
| | 1 egg, beaten | |
| 150ml/$\frac{1}{4}$ pint | milk | $\frac{5}{8}$ cup |

Grease and line a 17.5cm/7 inch round cake tin (pan). Sift the flour with the baking powder and salt into a mixing bowl. Add the fat and rub in with the fingertips until the mixture resembles coarse breadcrumbs. Stir in the sugar and coconut, then work in the egg and milk to give a soft dropping consistency. Turn the mixture into the prepared tin (pan), and level the surface.

Bake in a fairly hot oven, 190°C/375°F/Gas 5, for 50 minutes until risen and firm to the touch. Turn out on to a wire rack, and leave to cool.

**Note** The cake may be frosted with Coconut Frosting (see page 79).

# CORNISH HEAVY CAKE

| Metric/imperial | | American |
|---|---|---|
| 225g/8 oz | plain (all purpose) flour, sifted | 2 cups |
| | a pinch of salt | |
| 50g/2 oz | lard (shortening), diced | 4 tablespoons |
| 50g/2 oz | margarine, diced | 4 tablespoons |
| 50g/2 oz | sugar | $\frac{1}{4}$ cup |
| 75g/3 oz | currants | $\frac{1}{2}$ cup |
| 25g/1 oz | cut mixed peel (candied peel, chopped) | $\frac{1}{4}$ cup |
| 3 × 15ml spoons/ 3 tablespoons | water | 4 tablespoons |

Grease a baking sheet. Place the flour and salt in a mixing bowl. Add the fats, and rub in with the fingertips until the mixture resembles coarse breadcrumbs. Stir in the sugar, currants and peel. Add the water, and mix to a fairly stiff dough.

Knead gently until smooth, and shape into a round, about 1.25cm/$\frac{1}{2}$ inch thick. Place on the prepared baking sheet, and score the top into eight sections, using a sharp knife.

Bake in a fairly hot oven, 190°C/375°F/Gas 5, for 30 minutes until a skewer inserted into the centre of the cake comes out clean. Transfer to a wire rack, and leave to cool.

## Variation
For an attractive colour, add a good pinch of saffron powder to the mixture.

# WHOLEWHEAT CURRANT CAKE

| Metric/imperial | | American |
|---|---|---|
| 225g/8 oz | self-raising (self-rising) wholewheat flour | 2 cups |
| 1 × 5ml spoon/ 1 teaspoon | baking powder | 1 teaspoon |
| 100g/4 oz | butter **or** margarine, diced | 1 stick |
| 100g/4 oz | Demerara (brown) sugar | scant 1 cup, unpacked |
| | 2 eggs | |
| 7 × 15ml spoons/ 7 tablespoons | milk | 8 tablespoons |
| 225g/8 oz | currants | $1\frac{1}{3}$ cups |

Grease and base-line a 17.5cm/7 inch round cake tin (pan). Sift the flour with the baking powder into a mixing bowl. Add the fat, and rub in with the fingertips until the mixture resembles fine breadcrumbs. Stir in the sugar. Beat the eggs with the milk, and work into the mixture to give a soft dropping consistency. Stir in the currants until well mixed, then turn the mixture into the prepared tin (pan), and level the surface.

Bake in a warm oven, 160°C/325°F/Gas 3, for 1$\frac{1}{2}$ hours until risen and firm to the touch. Turn out on to a wire rack, and leave to cool.

*Wholewheat Currant Cake* **and** *Cornish Heavy Cake*

# VICTORIA SANDWICH

| Metric/imperial | | American |
|---|---|---|
| 100g/4 oz | butter **or** margarine | 1 stick |
| 100g/4 oz | caster (fine) sugar | ½ cup |
| 100g/4 oz | self-raising (self-rising) flour, sifted | 1 cup |
| | 2 eggs, beaten | |

### FILLING AND DECORATION

| | | |
|---|---|---|
| 2 × 15ml spoons/ 2 tablespoons | raspberry jam | 3 tablespoons |
| 1 × 15ml spoon/ 1 tablespoon | caster (fine) **or** icing (confectioner's) sugar, sifted | 1 tablespoon |

Grease and flour two 17.5cm/7 inch sandwich tins (layer pans). Cream together the fat and sugar until light, fluffy and pale. Gradually beat in the eggs, and fold in the flour. Divide the mixture equally between the prepared tins (pans), and level the surfaces.

Bake in a warm oven, 160°C/325°F/Gas 3, for 30 minutes until the tops spring back when pressed lightly. Turn the cakes out on to a wire rack, and leave to cool.

When cold, sandwich together with the jam, and sprinkle the top with the sugar.

**Note** For a pretty effect, place a paper doyly on top of the cake before sprinkling with icing sugar, then carefully lift away to leave a lacy pattern.

# MADEIRA CAKE

| Metric/imperial | | American |
|---|---|---|
| 100g/4 oz | butter | 1 stick |
| 100g/4 oz | caster (fine) sugar | ½ cup |
| 225g/8 oz | plain (all purpose) flour | 2 cups |
| 50g/2 oz | ground rice | ½ cup |
| 1 × 5ml spoon/ 1 teaspoon | cream of tartar | 1 teaspoon |
| 1 × 5ml spoon/ 1 teaspoon | bicarbonate of soda (baking soda) | 1 teaspoon |
| ½ × 2.5ml spoon/ ¼ teaspoon | salt | ¼ teaspoon |
| | 4 eggs, beaten | |
| | juice of ½ lemon | |

### DECORATION
a strip of
candied citron
peel

Grease and base-line a 17.5cm/7 inch round cake tin (pan). Cream together the butter and sugar until light, fluffy and pale. Sift the flour with the ground rice, cream of tartar, soda and salt. Fold the dry ingredients into the creamed mixture alternately with the eggs and lemon juice, a little at a time. Beat until smooth and creamy. Turn the mixture into the prepared tin (pan), and level the surface.

Bake in a moderate oven, 180°C/350°F/Gas 4, for 45 minutes. Very carefully open the oven door, and place the candied peel on top of the cake. Bake for a further 30 minutes until a skewer inserted into the centre of the cake comes out clean. Turn the cake out on to a wire rack, and leave to cool.

# MARMALADE SPONGE

| Metric/imperial | | American |
|---|---|---|
| 100g/4 oz | butter **or** margarine | 1 stick |
| 50g/2 oz | soft light brown sugar | ½ cup, unpacked |
| 2 × 15ml spoons/ 2 tablespoons | golden (light corn) syrup | 3 tablespoons |
| 100g/4 oz | self-raising (self-rising) flour | 1 cup |
| ½ × 2.5ml spoon/ ¼ teaspoon | baking powder | ¼ teaspoon |
| 1 × 2.5ml spoon/ ½ teaspoon | ground mixed spice | ½ teaspoon |
| | 2 eggs, beaten | |

### FILLING AND DECORATION

| | | |
|---|---|---|
| 75g/3 oz | coarse-cut orange marmalade | 4 tablespoons |
| 1 × 15ml spoon/ 1 tablespoon | icing (confectioner's) sugar, sifted | 1 tablespoon |

Grease and base-line two 17.5cm/7 inch sandwich tins (layer pans). Cream together the fat, sugar and syrup until light and fluffy. Sift the flour with the baking powder and spice. Gradually beat the eggs into the creamed mixture, folding in a little flour after each addition. Divide the mixture equally between the prepared tins (pans), and level the surfaces.

Bake in a fairly hot oven, 200°C/400°F/Gas 6, for 25 minutes until the tops spring back when pressed lightly. Turn out on to a wire rack, and leave to cool.

When cold, sandwich the cake together with the marmalade, and sprinkle the top with the icing (confectioner's) sugar.

# MARBLE CAKE

| Metric/imperial | | American |
|---|---|---|
| 225g/8 oz | butter **or** margarine | 2 sticks |
| 225g/8 oz | caster (fine) sugar | 1 cup |
| | 3 eggs, beaten | |
| | a few drops vanilla flavouring | |
| 275g/10 oz | self-raising (self-rising) flour, sifted | 2½ cups |
| 75g/3 oz | plain (semi-sweet) chocolate, broken into pieces | scant ¼ lb |

Grease and line a 17.5cm/7 inch round cake tin (pan). Cream together the fat and sugar until light, fluffy and pale. Gradually beat in the eggs, with the vanilla flavouring, folding in a little of the flour after each addition. Fold in the remaining flour.

Put half the mixture into a second bowl. Melt the chocolate in a bowl set over a saucepan of hot water, and stir into one of the bowls. Beat well until thoroughly combined. Place alternate spoonfuls of plain and chocolate mixture in the prepared tin, and level the surface.

Bake in a moderate oven, 180°C/350°F/Gas 4, for 45 minutes until the cake is well risen and firm to the touch. Turn out on to a wire rack, and leave to cool.

# MOCHA CAKE

| Metric/imperial | | American |
|---|---|---|
| 175g/6 oz | butter | 1½ sticks |
| 175g/6 oz | caster (fine) sugar | scant 1 cup |
| | 3 eggs, beaten | |
| 175g/6 oz | self-raising (self-rising) flour, sifted | 1½ cups |
| 2 × 15ml spoons/ 2 tablespoons | coffee essence (strong black coffee) | 3 tablespoons |
| 50g/2 oz | coarsely grated plain (semi-sweet) chocolate | ½ cup |
| | DECORATION | |
| 1 × 15ml spoon/ 1 tablespoon | icing (confectioner's) sugar, sifted | 1 tablespoon |

Grease and line a 20cm/8 inch round cake tin (pan). Cream together the butter and sugar until light, fluffy and pale. Gradually beat in the eggs, folding in a little of the flour after each addition. Fold in the remaining flour, then fold in the coffee essence and grated chocolate. Turn the mixture into the prepared tin (pan), and level the surface.

Bake in a moderate oven, 180°C/350°F/Gas 4, for 1½ hours until the cake is well risen and firm to the touch. Turn out on to a wire rack and leave to cool. Sprinkle the top with the icing (confectioner's) sugar.

# COFFEE WALNUT CAKE

| Metric/imperial | | American |
|---|---|---|
| 100g/4 oz | butter **or** margarine | 1 stick |
| 100g/4 oz | caster (fine) sugar | ½ cup |
| | 2 eggs, beaten | |
| 1 × 15ml spoon/ 1 tablespoon | coffee essence (strong black coffee) | 1 tablespoon |
| 100g/4 oz | self-raising (self-rising) flour, sifted | 1 cup |
| 50g/2 oz | shelled walnuts, chopped | ½ cup |
| | TOPPING AND DECORATION | |
| 100g/4 oz | icing (confectioner's) sugar, sifted | 1 cup |
| 2 × 5ml spoons/ 2 teaspoons | coffee essence | 3 teaspoons |
| | 12 walnut halves | |

Grease and base-line a deep 17.5cm/7 inch sandwich tin (layer pan). Cream together the fat and sugar until light, fluffy and pale. Gradually beat in the eggs. Stir in the coffee essence. Fold in the flour together with the walnuts. Turn the mixture into the prepared tin (pan), and level the surface.

Bake in a fairly hot oven, 190°C/375°F/Gas 5, for 25–30 minutes until the top springs back when pressed lightly. Turn the cake out on to a wire rack, and leave to cool.

To make the topping, place the icing (confectioner's) sugar in a bowl, and stir in the coffee essence and enough hot water to give a spreading consistency. Spread the icing over the top of the cake, and decorate with the walnut halves. Leave to set.

# HARVEST FRUIT CAKE

| Metric/imperial | | American |
|---|---|---|
| 100g/4 oz | butter **or** margarine | 1 stick |
| 100g/4 oz | sugar | $\frac{1}{2}$ cup |
| 225g/8 oz | self-raising (self-rising) flour | 2 cups |
| 1 × 2.5ml spoon/ $\frac{1}{2}$ teaspoon | ground ginger | $\frac{1}{2}$ teaspoon |
| 1 × 2.5ml spoon/ $\frac{1}{2}$ teaspoon | ground mixed spice | $\frac{1}{2}$ teaspoon |
| 1 × 5ml spoon/ 1 teaspoon | ground cinnamon | 1 teaspoon |
| 100g/4 oz | sultanas (golden raisins) | $\frac{3}{4}$ cup |
| 1 × 15ml spoon/ 1 tablespoon | vinegar | 1 tablespoon |
| 300ml/$\frac{1}{2}$ pint | apple purée | $1\frac{1}{4}$ cups |

Grease and line a 17.5cm/7 inch round cake tin (pan). Cream together the fat and sugar until light, fluffy and pale. Sift the flour with the spices, then fold into the creamed mixture. Stir in the sultanas (golden raisins), then the vinegar and apple purée. Turn the mixture into the prepared tin (pan), and level the surface.

Bake in a moderate oven, 180°C/350°F/Gas 4, for $1\frac{1}{2}$ hours until a skewer inserted into the centre of the cake comes out clean. Cool in the tin (pan) for a few minutes, then turn out on to a wire rack, and leave to cool completely.

# YOGHURT CAKE

| Metric/imperial | | American |
|---|---|---|
| 100g/4 oz | butter | 1 stick |
| 175g/6 oz | caster (fine) sugar | scant 1 cup |
| | finely grated rind of 1 lemon | |
| | 3 eggs, separated | |
| 175g/6 oz | self-raising (self-rising) flour, sifted | $1\frac{1}{2}$ cups |
| 175ml/6 fl oz | plain yoghurt | $\frac{3}{4}$ cup |
| 50g/2 oz | cut mixed peel (candied peel, chopped) | $\frac{1}{2}$ cup |

Grease and flour a 1kg/2 lb loaf tin (pan). Cream together the butter and sugar until light, fluffy and pale. Beat in the lemon rind. Beat in the egg yolks, one at a time, folding in a little of the flour after each addition. Fold in the remainder of the flour alternately with the yoghurt. Stir in the peel. Whisk the egg whites until stiff, then fold into the mixture. Turn into the prepared tin (pan), and level the surface.

Bake in a moderate oven, 180°C/350°F/Gas 4, for 1 hour until the cake is well risen and firm to the touch. Turn out on to a wire rack, and leave to cool.

### Variation
The cake may be covered with Lemon Glacé Icing (see page 73).

# CHERRY ALMOND CAKE

| Metric/imperial | | American |
|---|---|---|
| 175g/6 oz | glacé (candied) cherries, rinsed, dried and quartered | ¾ cup |
| 200g/7 oz | self-raising (self-rising) flour, sifted | 1¾ cups |
| 100g/4 oz | butter **or** margarine | 1 stick |
| 100g/4 oz | caster (fine) sugar | ½ cup |
| | 3 eggs, beaten | |
| 25g/1 oz | ground almonds | ¼ cup |

Grease and line a 15cm/6 inch round cake tin (pan). Toss the cherries in a little of the flour, to coat thoroughly. Cream together the fat and sugar until light, fluffy and pale. Gradually beat in the eggs, folding in a little of the flour after each addition. Stir in the ground almonds and cherries, and fold in the remaining flour. Turn the mixture into the prepared tin (pan), and level the surface.

Bake in a moderate oven, 180°C/350°F/Gas 4, for 1 hour 20 minutes until a skewer inserted into the centre of the cake comes out clean. Turn the cake out on to a wire rack, and leave to cool.

# OLD-FASHIONED SEED CAKE

| Metric/imperial | | American |
|---|---|---|
| 225g/8 oz | butter | 2 sticks |
| 225g/8 oz | caster (fine) sugar | 1 cup |
| | 4 eggs, beaten | |
| 225g/8 oz | plain (all purpose) flour, sifted | 2 cups |
| 3 × 5ml spoons/ 3 teaspoons | caraway seeds | 4 teaspoons |

Grease and line a 17.5cm/7 inch round cake tin (pan). Cream together the butter and all but 2 × 5ml spoons/2 teaspoons/3 US teaspoons of the sugar until light, fluffy and pale. Gradually beat in the eggs, folding in a little of the flour after each addition. Fold in the remaining flour and all but 1 × 2.5ml spoon/½ teaspoon of the caraway seeds. Turn the mixture into the prepared tin (pan), and level the surface. Sprinkle with the remaining sugar and caraway seeds.

Bake in a warm oven, 160°C/325°F/Gas 3, for 1¾ hours until a skewer inserted into the centre of the cake comes out clean. Cool in the tin (pan) for 10 minutes, then turn the cake out on to a wire rack, and leave to cool.

# DATE AND WALNUT CAKE

| Metric/imperial | | American |
|---|---|---|
| 175g/6 oz | butter **or** margarine | 1½ sticks |
| 175g/6 oz | soft light brown sugar | scant 1 cup, packed |
| 225g/8 oz | plain (all purpose) flour | 2 cups |
| 1½ × 5ml spoons/ 1½ teaspoons | baking powder | 2 teaspoons |
| | 3 eggs, beaten | |
| 50g/2 oz | shelled walnuts, chopped | ½ cup |
| 225g/8 oz | stoned dates, chopped | ½ lb |
| 2 × 15ml spoons/ 2 tablespoons | milk | 3 tablespoons |
| | **TOPPING** | |
| 50g/2 oz | unsalted butter **or** margarine | 4 tablespoons |
| 3 × 15ml spoons/ 3 tablespoons | milk | 4 tablespoons |
| 225g/8 oz | icing (confectioner's) sugar, sifted | 2 cups |
| 1 × 5ml spoon/ 1 teaspoon | coffee essence (strong black coffee) | 1 teaspoon |

Grease and line a 17.5cm/7 inch round cake tin (pan). Cream together the fat and sugar until light and fluffy. Sift the flour with the baking powder. Gradually beat the eggs into the creamed mixture, folding in a little of the flour after each addition. Beat well, then fold in the remaining flour, the walnuts, dates and milk. Turn the mixture into the prepared tin (pan), and level the surface.

Bake in a warm oven, 160°C/325°F/Gas 3, for 1½ hours until a skewer inserted into the centre of the cake comes out clean. Cool the cake in the tin (pan) for 10 minutes, then turn out on to a wire rack, and leave to cool completely.

To make the topping, place all the ingredients in a bowl set over a saucepan of gently simmering water, and stir until the mixture is melted and smooth. Remove from the heat and beat well until thick. Spread over the top and sides of the cake, and leave until set.

# GUINNESS (DARK BEER) CAKE

| Metric/imperial | | American |
|---|---|---|
| 225g/8 oz | butter | 2 sticks |
| 225g/8 oz | soft light brown sugar | 1½ cups, unpacked |
| | 4 eggs, beaten | |
| 300g/10 oz | plain (all purpose) flour | 2½ cups |
| 2 × 5ml spoons/ 2 teaspoons | ground mixed spice | 3 teaspoons |
| 225g/8 oz | seedless raisins | 1⅓ cups |
| 225g/8 oz | sultanas (golden raisins) | 1⅓ cups |
| 100g/4 oz | cut mixed peel (candied peel, chopped) | 1 cup |
| 100g/4 oz | walnuts, chopped | 1 cup |
| 8 × 15ml spoons/ 8 tablespoons | Guinness (dark beer) | 10 tablespoons |

Grease and base-line a 17.5cm/7 inch round cake tin (pan). Cream together the butter and sugar until light and fluffy. Gradually beat in the eggs, folding in a little sifted flour after each addition. Sift the remaining flour with the spice, and fold into the mixture. Add the raisins, sultanas (golden raisins), peel and walnuts, and stir well to mix. Stir in half the Guinness (dark beer). Turn the mixture into the prepared tin (pan), and level the surface.

Bake in a warm oven, 160°C/325°F/Gas 3, for 1 hour. Reduce the heat to cool, 150°C/300°F/Gas 2, and bake for a further 1½ hours until a skewer inserted into the centre of the cake comes out clean. Cool in the tin (pan) for 15 minutes, then turn out on to a wire rack. Prick the base of the cake all over with a skewer, and spoon over the remaining Guinness (dark beer). Leave to cool completely, then store in an airtight container for 1 week before serving.

# CHOCOLATE BANANA CAKE

| Metric/imperial | | American |
|---|---|---|
| 175g/6 oz | butter | 1½ sticks |
| 175g/6 oz | caster (fine) sugar | scant 1 cup |
| | 3 eggs, beaten | |
| 200g/7 oz | self-raising (self-rising) flour, sifted | 1¾ cups |
| 25g/1 oz | cocoa powder | ¼ cup |
| | 2 bananas, mashed | |

### FILLING AND TOPPING
1 recipe quantity Chocolate Buttercream (page 74)

1 recipe quantity Chocolate Glacé Icing (page 73)

banana slices

Grease and flour two 20cm/8 inch sandwich tins (layer pans). Cream together the butter and sugar until light, fluffy and pale. Gradually beat in the eggs, folding in a little of the flour after each addition. Fold in the remaining flour with the cocoa. Stir in the mashed bananas. Turn the mixture into the prepared tins (pans), and level the surfaces.

Bake in a fairly hot oven, 190°C/375°F/Gas 5, for 35 minutes until a skewer inserted into the centre of the cake comes out clean. Turn out on to a wire rack, and leave to cool.

When cold, sandwich the cakes together with the Chocolate Buttercream, and cover the top with Chocolate Glacé Icing. Decorate with the banana slices.

*Chocolate Banana Cake*

# DUTCH APPLE CAKE

| Metric/imperial | | American |
|---|---|---|
| 450g/1lb | cooking apples, peeled, cored and chopped | 1 lb |
| 3 × 15ml spoons/ 3 tablespoons | water | 4 tablespoons |
| 1 × 15ml spoon/ 1 tablespoon | sugar | 1 tablespoon |
| 75g/3 oz | unsalted butter | 6 tablespoons |
| 300g/11 oz | caster (fine) sugar | scant 1½ cups |
| 225g/8 oz | plain (all purpose) flour | 2 cups |
| 1 × 5ml spoon/ 1 teaspoon | baking powder | 1 teaspoon |
| ½ × 2.5ml spoon/ ¼ teaspoon | ground cinnamon | ¼ teaspoon |
| ½ × 2.5ml spoon/ ¼ teaspoon | ground nutmeg | ¼ teaspoon |
| ½ × 2.5ml spoon/ ¼ teaspoon | ground mixed spice | ¼ teaspoon |
| 1 × 5ml spoon/ 1 teaspoon | salt | 1 teaspoon |
| | 1 egg, beaten | |
| 50g/2 oz | shelled walnuts, chopped | ½ cup |
| 100g/4 oz | sultanas (golden raisins) | ¾ cup |
| 1 × 15ml spoon/ 1 tablespoon | DECORATION icing (confectioner's) sugar, sifted | 1 tablespoon |

Grease and base-line a 22.5cm/9 inch round cake tin (pan). Place the apples in a saucepan with the water and 1 × 15ml spoon/1 tablespoon sugar, and simmer, stirring occasionally, until soft and pulpy. Remove from the heat, beat well and allow to cool.

Cream together the butter and caster (fine) sugar until light, fluffy and pale. Sift the flour with the baking powder, spices and salt. Beat the egg into the creamed mixture, folding in the flour, a little at a time, with the apple purée, walnuts and sultanas (golden raisins). Turn the mixture into the prepared tin (pan), and level the surface.

Bake in a moderate oven, 180°C/350°F/Gas 4, for 1¼ hours until a skewer inserted into the centre of the cake comes out clean. Cool in the tin (pan) for a few minutes, then turn out on to a wire rack, and leave to cool completely. Sprinkle the top with the icing (confectioner's) sugar.

# DUNDEE CAKE

| Metric/imperial | | American |
|---|---|---|
| 175g/6 oz | butter | 1½ sticks |
| 190g/6½ oz | sugar | scant 1 cup |
| 225g/8 oz | plain (all purpose) flour | 2 cups |
| | a pinch of salt | |
| 1 × 5ml spoon/ 1 teaspoon | baking powder | 1 teaspoon |
| | 3 eggs, beaten | |
| 1 × 15ml spoon/ 1 tablespoon | ground almonds | 1 tablespoon |
| 225g/8 oz | sultanas (golden raisins) | 1⅓ cups |
| 225g/8 oz | currants | 1⅓ cups |
| 75g/3 oz | cut mixed peel (candied peel, chopped) | ¾ cup |
| 75g/3 oz | glacé (candied) cherries, rinsed, dried and quartered | scant ½ cup |
| | finely grated rind and juice of ½ lemon | |
| 1 × 15ml spoon/ 1 tablespoon | brandy | 1 tablespoon |
| 50g/2 oz | blanched split almonds | ½ cup |
| 2 × 15ml spoons/ 2 tablespoons | milk | 3 tablespoons |

Grease and base-line a 20cm/8 inch round cake tin (pan). Cream together the butter and 175g/6 oz/scant US cup of the sugar until light, fluffy and pale. Sift the flour with the salt and baking powder. Gradually beat the eggs into the creamed mixture, folding in a little of the flour after each addition. Stir in the ground almonds, sultanas (golden raisins), currants, peel and cherries, then stir in the lemon rind and juice. Fold in any remaining flour with the brandy. Turn the mixture into the prepared tin (pan), and level the surface.

Cover with foil and bake in a cool oven, 150°C/300°F/Gas 2, for 1½ hours. Remove the foil and arrange the almonds on top of the cake. Bake for 1 further hour until a skewer inserted into the centre of the cake comes out clean.

Stir together the milk and the remaining sugar, and brush over the top of the cake. Bake for a further 5 minutes. Cool in the tin (pan) for 1 hour, then turn out on to a wire rack, and leave to cool completely.

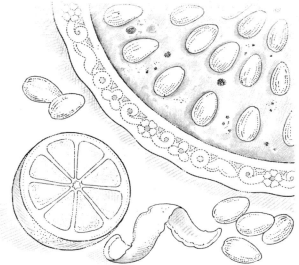

# CARROT CAKE

| Metric/imperial | | American |
|---|---|---|
| 100g/4 oz | butter **or** margarine | 1 stick |
| 100g/4 oz | soft dark brown sugar | scant 1 cup, unpacked |
| 100g/4 oz | plain (all purpose) flour | 1 cup |
| 1 × 5ml spoon/ 1 teaspoon | baking powder | 1 teaspoon |
| 1 × 2.5ml spoon/ ½ teaspoon | bicarbonate of soda (baking soda) | ½ teaspoon |
| | 2 eggs, beaten | |
| 100g/4 oz | carrots, finely grated | ¼ lb |
| 100g/4 oz | seedless raisins | 1 cup |
| 50g/2 oz | walnuts, chopped | ½ cup |
| | FROSTING | |
| 350g/12 oz | cream cheese | ¾ lb |
| 2 × 5ml spoons/ 2 teaspoons | lemon juice | 2 teaspoons |
| 50g/2 oz | icing (confectioner's) sugar, sifted | ½ cup |
| | 8 walnut halves | |

Grease and base-line two 17.5cm/7 inch sandwich tins (layer pans). Cream together the fat and sugar until light and fluffy. Sift the flour with the baking powder and soda. Gradually beat the eggs into the creamed mixture, folding in a little of the flour after each addition. Fold in the remaining flour, then the carrots, raisins and walnuts. Divide the mixture equally between the prepared tins (pans), and level the surfaces.

Bake in a moderate oven, 180°C/350°F/Gas 4, for 40 minutes until risen and firm to the touch. Turn the cakes out on to a wire rack, and leave to cool completely.

To make the frosting, beat the cream cheese with the lemon juice and icing (confectioner's) sugar until light and creamy. Use a little to sandwich the cakes together. Swirl the remaining frosting around the top and sides of the cake, and decorate with the walnut halves. Leave to set.

# FATLESS SPONGE

| Metric/imperial | | American |
|---|---|---|
| | 4 eggs | |
| 100g/4 oz | caster (fine) sugar | ½ cup |
| | a pinch of salt | |
| 100g/4 oz | plain (all purpose) flour, sifted | 1 cup |

### FILLING AND DECORATION

| | | |
|---|---|---|
| 3 × 15ml spoons/ 3 tablespoons | apricot jam | 4 tablespoons |
| 1 × 15ml spoon/ 1 tablespoon | caster (fine) **or** icing (confectioner's) sugar, sifted | 1 tablespoon |

Grease and flour two 20cm/8 inch sandwich tins (layer pans). Whisk together the eggs, sugar and salt until light, thick and creamy. Fold in the flour. Divide the mixture equally between the prepared tins (pans), and level the surfaces.

Bake in a hot oven, 200°C/400°F/Gas 6, for 20 minutes until the tops spring back when pressed lightly. Turn the cakes out on to a wire rack, and leave to cool completely.

When cold, sandwich the cakes together with the jam, and sprinkle the top with the sugar.

# CORNFLOUR SPONGE

| Metric/imperial | | American |
|---|---|---|
| | 3 eggs | |
| 75g/3 oz | caster (fine) sugar | scant ½ cup |
| 75g/3 oz | plain (all purpose) flour | ¾ cup |
| 25g/1 oz | cornflour (cornstarch) | ¼ cup |
| 1 × 5ml spoon/ 1 teaspoon | baking powder | 1 teaspoon |
| | a pinch of salt | |
| 25g/1 oz | butter, melted | 2 tablespoons |
| 3 × 15ml spoons/ 3 tablespoons | hot water | 4 tablespoons |

### FILLING AND DECORATION

| | | |
|---|---|---|
| 3 × 15ml spoons/ 3 tablespoons | raspberry jam | 4 tablespoons |
| 1 × 15ml spoon/ 1 tablespoon | icing (confectioner's) sugar, sifted | 1 tablespoon |

Grease two 17.5cm/7 inch sandwich tins (layer pans). Whisk the eggs with the sugar until light and pale. Sift the flour with the cornflour (cornstarch), baking powder and salt, and fold into the egg mixture, then fold in the butter and water. Turn into the prepared tins (pans), and level the surfaces.

Bake in a fairly hot oven, 190°C/375°F/Gas 5, for 20 minutes until risen and the tops spring back when pressed lightly. Turn out on to a wire rack, and leave to cool completely.

Sandwich the cakes together with the jam, and sprinkle the top with icing (confectioner's) sugar.

# FEATHERLIGHT SPONGE CAKE

| Metric/imperial | | American |
|---|---|---|
| | 3 eggs, separated | |
| 150g/5 oz | caster (fine) sugar | scant $\frac{3}{4}$ cup |
| 75g/3 oz | plain (all purpose) flour, sifted | $\frac{3}{4}$ cup |
| | DECORATION | |
| 1 × 15ml spoon/ 1 tablespoon | caster (fine) **or** (confectioner's) sugar, sifted | 1 tablespoon |

Grease and base-line a 20cm/8 inch round cake tin (pan). Whisk the egg whites in a mixing bowl until very stiff. Set the bowl over a saucepan of hot, but not boiling water, making sure that the base of the bowl does not touch the water. Gradually beat in the egg yolks and sugar, then beat for 5 minutes. Very lightly fold in the flour, then turn the mixture into the prepared tin (pan), and level the surface.

Bake in a hot oven, 200°C/400°F/Gas 6, for 45 minutes until the top springs back when pressed lightly. Turn the cake out on to a wire rack, and leave to cool.

When cold, sprinkle the top with the sugar.

# SWISS ROLL (JELLY ROLL)

| Metric/imperial | | American |
|---|---|---|
| | 3 eggs | |
| 175g/6 oz | caster (fine) sugar | scant 1 cup |
| 75g/3 oz | plain (all purpose) flour | $\frac{3}{4}$ cup |
| 1 × 2.5ml spoon/ $\frac{1}{2}$ teaspoon | baking powder | $\frac{1}{2}$ teaspoon |
| 1 × 15ml spoon/ 1 tablespoon | cold water | 1 tablespoon |
| | FILLING | |
| 3 × 15ml spoons/ 3 tablespoons | raspberry jam, warmed | 4 tablespoons |

Grease and line a 33.5 × 22.5cm/13 × 9 inch Swiss Roll tin (jelly roll pan). Whisk together the eggs and 115g/4½ oz/½ US cup of the sugar until light, thick and creamy. Sift the flour with the baking powder, and fold into the mixture with the water. Turn into the prepared tin (pan), and level the surface.

Bake in a hot oven, 200°C/400°F/Gas 6, for 10 minutes until the top springs back when pressed lightly.

Turn out on to a sheet of greaseproof paper or clean tea-towel sprinkled with half the remaining sugar. Trim the edges with a sharp knife, then spread quickly with the jam. Roll up tightly from one short end, then leave to cool completely on a wire rack. Sprinkle with the remaining sugar.

### Variation
Lemon curd may be substituted for the raspberry jam.

# ORANGE JUICE CAKE

| Metric/imperial | | American |
|---|---|---|
| | 5 eggs, separated | |
| 200g/7 oz | caster (fine) sugar | scant 1 cup |
| 225g/8 oz | plain (all purpose) flour | 2 cups |
| | a pinch of salt | |
| 2 × 5ml spoons/ 2 teaspoons | baking powder | 3 teaspoons |
| 1 × 5ml spoon/ 1 teaspoon | lemon juice | 1 teaspoon |
| scant 150ml/ ¼ pint | orange juice | ½ cup |

DECORATION
1 recipe quantity
Orange Glacé
Icing (page 73)

crystallized
orange slices

Grease and flour a 20cm/8 inch round cake tin (pan). Beat the egg yolks until foamy. Add half the sugar, and beat again until the sugar has dissolved. Sift the flour with the salt and baking powder, and fold into the yolk mixture, alternately with the fruit juices. Whisk the egg whites until they form stiff peaks, then fold in the remaining sugar, and whisk again. Fold into the cake mixture. Turn into the prepared tin (pan), and level the surface.

Bake in a moderate oven, 180°C/350°F/Gas 4, for 1 hour until well risen and firm to the touch. Turn the cake out on to a wire rack, and leave to cool. Cover with the glacé icing, and decorate with crystallized orange slices.

# GENOESE SPONGE

| Metric/imperial | | American |
|---|---|---|
| | 4 eggs | |
| 100g/4 oz | caster (fine) sugar | ½ cup |
| 75g/3 oz | plain (all purpose) flour, sifted | ¾ cup |
| 75g/3 oz | butter, melted | 6 tablespoons |
| | DECORATION | |
| 1 × 15ml spoon/ 1 tablespoon | caster (fine) **or** icing (confectioner's) sugar, sifted | 1 tablespoon |

Grease and flour a 20cm/8 inch sandwich tin (layer pan). Beat together the eggs and sugar in a bowl set over hot, but not boiling, water until light, thick and creamy, making sure the base of the bowl does not touch the water. Remove the bowl from the heat, and beat for a further 3 minutes. Very lightly fold in half the flour and the butter. Very gently fold in the remaining flour. Turn the mixture into the prepared tin (pan), and level the surface.

Bake in a hot oven, 200°C/400°F/Gas 6, for 30 minutes until firm to the touch. Allow to cool in the tin (pan) for a few minutes, then turn out on to a wire rack and leave to cool completely.

When cold, sprinkle the top with the sugar.

Variation
The sponge may also be iced with Glacé Icing (see page 73).

*Marmalade Sponge (page 15)* **and** *Orange Juice Cake*

# Dorset Gingerbread

| Metric/imperial | | American |
|---|---|---|
| 225g/8 oz | butter **or** margarine | 2 sticks |
| 225g/8 oz | soft light brown sugar | 1½ cups, unpacked |
| 225g/8 oz | black treacle (molasses) | ⅔ cup |
| 350g/12 oz | plain (all purpose) flour | 3 cups |
| 4 × 5ml spoons/ 4 teaspoons | ground ginger | 5 teaspoons |
| 3 × 5ml spoons/ 3 teaspoons | ground cinnamon | 4 teaspoons |
| | 2 eggs, beaten | |
| 300ml/½ pint | milk | 1¼ cups |
| 2 × 5ml spoons/ 2 teaspooons | bicarbonate of soda (baking soda) | 3 teaspoons |

Grease and line a 27.5 × 17.5cm/11 × 7 inch tin (pan). Gently heat together the fat, sugar and treacle until just warm and melted. Sift the flour with the spices, and stir into the melted mixture alternately with the beaten eggs. Beat the mixture well. Warm the milk just to blood heat, then stir in the soda. Add to the mixture, beat well again, turn into the prepared tin (pan), and level the surface.

Bake in a warm oven, 160°C/325°F/Gas 3, for 1½ hours until a skewer inserted into the centre of the cake comes out clean. Cool in the tin (pan) for 5 minutes, then turn out on to a wire rack, and leave to cool.

# Syrup Sponge

| Metric/imperial | | American |
|---|---|---|
| 50g/2 oz | butter | 4 tablespoons |
| 50g/2 oz | sugar | ¼ cup |
| 4 × 15ml spoons/ 4 tablespoons | golden (light corn) syrup | 5 tablespoons |
| | 1 egg, beaten | |
| 2 × 15ml spoons/ 2 tablespoons | milk | 3 tablespoons |
| 100g/4 oz | self-raising (self-rising) flour, sifted | 1 cup |

Grease a 20cm/8 inch sandwich tin (layer pan). Melt the butter with the sugar and syrup in a saucepan over gentle heat, then leave to cool slightly.

Beat the egg with the milk, and add to the melted mixture alternately with the flour. Mix well, then turn into the prepared tin (pan), and level the surface.

Bake in a moderate oven, 180°C/350°F/Gas 4, for 35 minutes until risen and firm to the touch. Turn out on to a wire rack, and leave to cool.

### Variation
The cake may be iced with Lemon Glacé Icing (see page 73).

# Yorkshire Moggie Cake

| Metric/imperial | | American |
|---|---|---|
| 450g/1 lb | plain (all purpose) flour | 4 cups |
| 2 × 5ml spoons/ 2 teaspoons | baking powder | 3 teaspoons |
| 225g/8 oz | caster (fine) sugar | 1 cup |
| 225g/8 oz | black treacle (molasses) | ⅔ cup |
| 175g/6 oz | butter, diced | 1½ sticks |
| 150ml/¼ pint | milk | ⅝ cup |
| | 1 egg, beaten | |

Grease and base-line a 27.5 × 17.5cm/11 × 7 inch tin (pan). Sift the flour with the baking powder into a mixing bowl, and stir in the sugar. Gently heat together the treacle (molasses), butter and milk until just warm and melted. Stir into the dry ingredients, and beat in the egg. Beat the mixture well, then turn into the prepared tin (pan), and level the surface.

Bake in a warm oven, 160°C/325°F/Gas 3, for 1½ hours until a skewer inserted into the centre of the cake comes out clean. Cool in the tin (pan) for 5 minutes, then turn out on to a wire rack, and leave to cool completely. Serve cut into squares.

# Wholewheat Dripping Cake

| Metric/imperial | | American |
|---|---|---|
| 225g/8 oz | mixed dried fruit | 1⅓ cups |
| 75g/3 oz | beef dripping | 6 tablespoons |
| 150g/5 oz | soft light brown sugar | 1 cup, unpacked |
| 215ml/7½ fl oz | water | scant 1 cup |
| 225g/8 oz | plain wholewheat flour | 2 cups |
| 1 × 5ml spoon/ 1 teaspoon | baking powder | 1 teaspoon |
| | a pinch of ground nutmeg | |
| | a pinch of ground cinnamon | |
| | a pinch of ground mixed spice | |
| 1 × 2.5ml spoon/ ½ teaspoon | bicarbonate of soda (baking soda) | ½ teaspoon |

Grease and line a 17.5cm/7 inch round cake tin (pan). Place the dried fruit, dripping, sugar and water in a saucepan. Bring to the boil, then simmer for 10 minutes, stirring frequently. Remove from the heat and leave to cool.

Sift the flour with the baking powder, spices and soda. Stir into the dried fruit mixture, and mix well, but do not beat. Turn the mixture into the prepared tin (pan), and level the surface.

Bake in a moderate oven, 180°C/350°F/Gas 4, for 1½ hours until a skewer inserted into the centre of the cake comes out clean. Cool in the tin (pan) for 5 minutes, then turn out on to a wire rack, and leave to cool.

# ALL-IN-ONE RICH FRUIT CAKE

| Metric/imperial | | American |
|---|---|---|
| 250g/9 oz | plain (all purpose) flour, sifted | 2¼ cups |
| 2 × 5ml spoons/ 2 teaspoons | baking powder | 3 teaspoons |
| 1 × 5ml spoon/ 1 teaspoon | ground nutmeg | 1 teaspoon |
| 1 × 5ml spoon/ 1 teaspoon | ground mixed spice | 1 teaspoon |
| 225g/8 oz | soft margarine | ½ lb |
| 225g/8 oz | soft light brown sugar | 1½ cups, unpacked |
| | 5 eggs | |
| | finely grated rind of 1 lemon | |
| 100g/4 oz | glacé (candied) cherries, rinsed, dried and quartered | ½ cup |
| 100g/4 oz | cut mixed peel (candied peel, chopped) | 1 cup |
| 50g/2 oz | ground almonds | ½ cup |
| 2 × 15ml spoons/ 2 tablespoons | brandy | 3 tablespoons |
| 1 × 15ml spoon/ 1 tablespoon | black treacle (molasses) | 1 tablespoon |
| 225g/8 oz | currants | 1⅓ cups |
| 225g/8 oz | sultanas (golden raisins) | 1⅓ cups |
| 225g/8 oz | raisins | 1⅓ cups |

Grease and line a 22.5cm/9 inch round cake tine (pan). Sift the flour with the baking powder and spices. Place all the ingredients in a mixing bowl, and beat for about 4 minutes until thoroughly mixed. Turn the mixture into the prepared tin (pan), and level the surface.

Bake in a cool oven, 140°C/275°F/Gas 1, for 5 hours until a skewer inserted into the centre of the cake comes out clean. Cool in the tin (pan) for 5 minutes, then turn out on to a wire rack, and leave to cool.

# ALL-IN-ONE SANDWICH CAKE

| Metric/imperial | | American |
|---|---|---|
| 100g/4 oz | soft margarine | ¼ lb |
| 100g/4 oz | caster (fine) sugar | ½ cup |
| | 2 eggs | |
| 100g/4 oz | self-raising (self-rising) flour, sifted | 1 cup |
| 1 × 5ml spoon/ 1 teaspoon | baking powder | 1 teaspoon |

### FILLING AND DECORATION

| | | |
|---|---|---|
| 3 × 15ml spoons/ 3 tablespoons | strawberry jam | 4 tablespoons |
| 1 × 15ml spoon/ 1 tablespoon | icing (confectioner's) sugar, sifted | 1 tablespoon |

Grease and base-line a 20cm/8 inch deep sandwich tin (layer pan). Place all the ingredients in a mixing bowl, and beat for about 3 minutes until smooth and thoroughly combined. Turn the mixture into the prepared tin (pan), and level the surface.

Bake in a moderate oven, 180°C/350°F/Gas 4, for 35 minutes until the top springs back when pressed lightly. Turn the cake out on to a wire rack, and leave to cool.

Split the cake in half, and sandwich together with the jam. Sprinkle the top with the icing (confectioner's) sugar.

## Variations

**Chocolate Sandwich Cake**

Add 25g/1oz/¼ US cup cocoa powder mixed with 2 × 15ml spoons/2 tablespoons/3 US tablespoons hot water to the cake mixture. Fill and cover with Chocolate Buttercream (see page 74).

**Coffee Sandwich Cake**

Add 1 × 15ml spoon/1 tablespoon coffee essence (strong black coffee) to the cake mixture. Fill and cover with Coffee Buttercream (see page 74).

**Lemon or Orange Sandwich Cake**

Add 2 × 5ml spoons/2 teaspoons/3 US teaspoons finely grated lemon or orange rind to the cake mixture. Fill and cover with Lemon or Orange Buttercream (see page 74).

# SPECIAL OCCASION CAKES

## PRALINE CREAM GÂTEAU

| Metric/imperial | | American |
|---|---|---|
| 225g/8 oz | butter | 2 sticks |
| 225g/8 oz | caster (fine) sugar | 1 cup |
| | 4 eggs, beaten | |
| 275g/10 oz | plain (all purpose) flour | 2½ cups |
| 2 × 5ml spoons/ 2 teaspoons | baking powder | 3 teaspoons |
| 25g/1 oz | ground almonds | ¼ cup |
| 2 × 15ml spoons/ 2 tablespoons | water | 3 tablespoons |

### FILLING AND TOPPING

| | | |
|---|---|---|
| 25g/1 oz | ground almonds | ¼ cup |
| 150g/5 oz | sugar | ¾ cup |
| 165ml/5½ fl oz | water | ¾ cup |
| | 3 egg yolks | |
| 450ml/¾ pint | double (heavy) cream, whipped | scant 2 cups |
| 2 × 15ml spoons/ 2 tablespoons | apricot jam, sieved | 3 tablespoons |
| 65g/2½ oz | blanched almonds | generous ½ cup |

Grease and line a 25cm/10 inch round cake tin (pan). Cream together the butter and sugar until light, fluffy and pale. Beat in the eggs, one at a time. Sift the flour with the baking powder, stir in the ground almonds and gradually fold into the creamed mixture, adding a little of the water after each addition. Turn the mixture into the prepared tin (pan).

Bake in a moderate oven, 180°C/350°F/Gas 4, for 1¼ hours until the cake is well risen and firm to the touch. Turn out on to a wire rack, and leave to cool.

To make the praline cream filling, spread the ground almonds out on a baking sheet, and heat in a moderate oven, 180°C/350°F/Gas 4, for 5–10 minutes until golden-brown. (Watch the almonds carefully, as they catch very easily.) Remove from the oven and leave to cool.

Heat 100g/4 oz/½ US cup of the sugar with 150ml/¼ pint/⅝ US cup of the water to 102°C/247°F, or until a little of the syrup dropped into a cup of cold water forms a large firm ball when rolled between finger and thumb.

Whisk the sugar syrup into the egg yolks, then whisk in the roasted ground almonds. Heat the remaining sugar and water until it turns a deep golden caramel. Whisk into the egg yolk mixture until it thickens and cools. Leave until cold, then fold in one-third of the whipped cream.

Split the cake in half, and spread the lower half with apricot jam. Spread over a thick layer of praline cream, and place the top layer of cake on top. Coat the sides of the cake with half the remaining jam, then with half the remaining whipped cream.

Chop 50g/2 oz/½ US cup of the blanched almonds and split the remainder. Spread the split almonds out on a baking sheet, and roast in a moderate oven, 180°C/350°F/Gas 4, until golden. Spread the chopped almonds on a sheet of greaseproof paper, and roll the sides of the cake in the nuts until coated. Place the cake on a serving plate.

Spread the top of the cake with the remaining jam and praline cream. Pipe the remaining cream in rosettes round the edge of the cake. Decorate with the split roasted almonds.

34

# FRUIT SAVARIN

| Metric/imperial | | American |
|---|---|---|
| 25g/1oz | fresh (compressed) yeast | 2 × 18g cakes |
| | **or** | |
| 15g/½oz | conventional dried (active dry) yeast | 2 × ¼oz packages |
| 6 × 15ml spoons/ 6 tablespoons | warm milk | 7 tablespoons |
| 225g/8oz | strong (bread) flour, sifted | 2 cups |
| 1 × 2.5ml spoon/ ½ teaspoon | salt | ½ teaspoon |
| 25g/1oz | caster (fine) sugar | 3 tablespoons |
| | 4 eggs, beaten | |
| 100g/4oz | butter, softened | 1 stick |
| | **RUM SYRUP** | |
| 550g/1¼lb | sugar | 3 cups |
| 600ml/1 pint | water | 2½ cups |
| 8 × 15ml spoons/ 8 tablespoons | rum | 9 tablespoons |
| | **DECORATION** | |
| 5 × 15ml spoons/ 5 tablespoons | apricot jam, warmed and sieved | 6 tablespoons |
| 225g/8oz | strawberries, halved | ½ lb |
| 100g/4oz | white grapes, halved and de-seeded | ¼ lb |
| | 2 slices pineapple, cut into 1.25cm/½ inch chunks | |
| 150ml/¼ pint | double (heavy) cream, whipped | ⅝ cup |

Grease a 20–22.5cm/8–9 inch ovenproof ring mould (pan). In a large mixing bowl, mix together the yeast, milk and 50g/2oz/ ½ US cup of the flour until smooth. Leave to stand until frothy. Add the remaining flour, the salt, sugar, eggs and butter, and beat vigorously for 3–4 minutes.

Half fill the prepared ring mould (pan) with the dough. Place it inside a large oiled polythene bag, and leave to prove in a warm place until the dough almost reaches the top of the mould (pan) (about 30–40 minutes).

Bake in a hot oven, 200°C/400°F/Gas 6, for 20–25 minutes, until a deep golden-brown.

Meanwhile, to make the rum syrup, place the sugar and water in a heavy-based saucepan, and heat gently until dissolved. Bring to the boil and boil for 1 minute. Remove from the heat and stir in the rum.

Remove the savarin from the oven, and leave to cool in the tin (pan) for 5 minutes, then turn out on to a wire rack set over a plate. Prick all over with a fine skewer. Pour over all but 150ml/ ¼ pint/⅝ US cup of the hot rum syrup, then spoon over again any of the syrup that drains into the plate. Place the savarin on a serving plate, and brush with the jam.

Mix the fruit with the reserved syrup. Pile into the centre of the savarin, and decorate with piped cream.

# CIDER SYRUP GÂTEAU

| Metric/imperial | | American |
|---|---|---|
| | 6 eggs, separated | |
| 175g/6 oz | caster (fine) sugar | scant 1 cup |
| 175g/6 oz | plain (all purpose) flour | 1½ cups |
| | CIDER SYRUP | |
| 150ml/¼ pint | sweet cider | ⅝ cup |
| 100g/4 oz | caster (fine) sugar | ½ cup |
| | FILLING AND DECORATION | |
| 25g/1 oz | icing (confectioner's) sugar, sifted | ¼ cup |
| 600ml/1 pint | double (heavy) **or** whipping cream, whipped stiffly | 2½ cups |
| 1 × 5ml spoon/ 1 teaspoon | rum | 1 teaspoon |
| | strips of orange rind | |

Grease and base-line two 20cm/8 inch sandwich tins (layer pans). Whisk the egg whites until they form stiff peaks. Whisk in the egg yolks alternately with the sugar. Sift the flour over the mixture, and fold in. Divide the mixture evenly between the prepared tins (pans), and level the surfaces.

Bake in a hot oven, 200°C/400°F/Gas 6, for 20 minutes until the tops spring back when pressed lightly. Turn out on to a wire rack, and leave to cool.

To make the syrup, place the cider and sugar in a heavy-based saucepan, and heat gently until dissolved. Bring to the boil and boil until reduced by half. Cool, then pour over the sponges.

To make the filling and decoration, fold the icing (confectioner's) sugar into the cream, and stir in the rum. Use one-quarter to sandwich the cakes together, then spread most of the remaining cream on top and use the remainder to pipe rosettes round the edge. Decorate with the orange rind.

# APPLE AND RAISIN GÂTEAU

| Metric/imperial | | American |
|---|---|---|
| 450ml/¾ pint | sweet cider | scant 2 cups |
| 150g/5 oz | sugar | scant ¾ cup |
| 100g/4 oz | seedless raisins | ¾ cup |
| | 3 eggs | |
| 75g/3 oz | caster (fine) sugar | scant ½ cup |
| 65g/2½ oz | plain (all purpose) flour, sifted | scant ¾ cup |
| | 1 apple, peeled, cored and sliced | |
| 5 × 15ml spoons/ 5 tablespoons | double (heavy) **or** whipping cream, whipped | 6 tablespoons |

Place 300ml/½ pint/1¼ US cups of the cider in a saucepan with 100g/4 oz/½ US cup sugar and the raisins, bring to the boil, and boil until reduced by half. Cool, cover and leave overnight.

Grease two 17.5cm/7 inch sandwich tins (layer pans). Whisk the eggs with the caster (fine) sugar in a bowl set over a saucepan of gently simmering water until thick and creamy. Remove the bowl from the pan, and continue to whisk until cold. Gradually fold in the flour, then turn the mixture into the prepared tins (pans) and level the surfaces.

Bake in a fairly hot oven, 190°C/375°F/Gas 5, for 15 minutes until risen and the tops spring back when pressed lightly. Leave to cool in the tins (pans) for 5 minutes, then turn out on to a wire rack.

Using a slotted spoon, remove the raisins from the cider syrup. Poach the apple slices in the remaining cider and sugar until just tender. Drain and cool.

Brush one of the cakes with the cider syrup, spread with the cream, and sprinkle with the raisins. Cover with the second sponge cake, brush with more syrup, and arrange the apple slices on top. Brush with the remaining syrup.

*Cider Syrup Gâteau* **and** *Apple and Raisin Gâteau*

# COFFEE FRUIT LOG

| Metric/imperial | | American |
|---|---|---|
| 100g/4 oz | self-raising (self-rising) flour | 1 cup |
| 1 × 5ml spoon/ 1 teaspoon | baking powder | 1 teaspoon |
| 1 × 2.5ml spoon/ ½ teaspoon | salt | ½ teaspoon |
| | 2 eggs, beaten | |
| 100g/4 oz | soft margarine | ¼ lb |
| 175g/6 oz | mixed dried fruit | 1 cup |
| 25g/1 oz | cut mixed peel (candied peel, chopped) | ¼ cup |
| 25g/1 oz | glacé (candied) cherries, rinsed, dried and quartered | 3 tablespoons |
| COATING AND DECORATION | | |
| 100g/4 oz | unsalted butter **or** margarine | 1 stick |
| 225g/8 oz | icing (confectioner's) sugar, sifted | 2 cups |
| 2 × 15ml spoons/ 2 tablespoons | coffee essence (strong black coffee) | 3 tablespoons |
| 15g/½ oz | flaked (slivered) almonds, toasted | 2 tablespoons |

Grease and line a 32.5 × 22.5cm/13 × 9 inch Swiss roll tin (jelly roll pan). Sift the flour with the baking powder and salt into a mixing bowl. Add the eggs and margarine, and stir well to mix, then beat vigorously for 2–3 minutes. Mix in the dried fruit, peel and cherries. Turn the mixture into the prepared tin (pan), and level the surface.

Bake in a moderate oven, 180°C/350°F/Gas 4, for 25–30 minutes until firm to the touch. Cool in the tin for 1 minute, then turn out on to a sheet of greaseproof paper, oiled on both sides. Roll up with the paper inside. Transfer to a wire rack, and leave to cool.

To make the coating, cream the fat until soft, then gradually beat in the icing (confectioner's) sugar until light and fluffy. Beat in the coffee essence.

Unroll the sponge very carefully. Spread with a little of the buttercream, then roll up tightly from one short end. Spread the cake with the remaining buttercream, and mark in lines with a fork to resemble a log. Decorate with the almonds.

**Note** This cake is best made a day in advance.

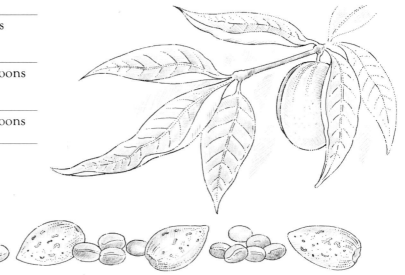

# WHISKY MOCHA CAKE

| Metric/imperial | | American |
|---|---|---|
| 75g/3 oz | self-raising (self-rising) flour | ¾ cup |
| 15g/½ oz | cornflour (cornstarch) | 3 tablespoons |
| 15g/½ oz | cocoa powder | 3 tablespoons |
| 15g/½ oz | instant coffee powder | 3 tablespoons |
| 1 × 5ml spoon/ 1 teaspoon | baking powder | 1 teaspoon |
| 100g/4 oz | soft margarine | ¼ lb |
| 100g/4 oz | caster (fine) sugar | ½ cup |
| | 2 eggs, beaten | |
| 1 × 5ml spoon/ 1 teaspoon | whisky | 1 teaspoon |
| | **TOPPING** | |
| 50g/2 oz | unsalted butter, softened | 4 tablespoons |
| 100g/4 oz | icing (confectioner's) sugar, sifted | 1 cup |
| 2 × 5ml spoons/ 2 teaspoons | whisky | 3 teaspoons |
| 1 × 5ml spoon/ 1 teaspoon | coffee essence (strong black coffee) | 1 teaspoon |
| | **DECORATION** | |
| 50g/2 oz | grated plain (semi-sweet) chocolate | ½ cup |

Grease and base-line two 17.5cm/7 inch sandwich tins (layer pans). Sift the flour with the cornflour (cornstarch), cocoa, coffee and baking powder. Cream the margarine with the sugar in a mixing bowl until light, fluffy and pale, then beat in the eggs, a little at a time, folding in a little of the flour mixture after each addition. Fold in the remaining flour mixture with the whisky. Turn the mixture into the prepared tins (pans), and level the surfaces.

Bake in a warm oven, 160°C/325°F/Gas 3, for 30 minutes until risen and firm to the touch. Turn out on to a wire rack, and leave to cool completely.

To make the topping, cream together all the ingredients. Use half the mixture to sandwich the cakes together, then spread the remainder on top, and sprinkle with the chocolate. Leave to set.

# COFFEE GÂTEAU

| Metric/imperial | | American |
|---|---|---|
| | two 17.5cm/7 inch Victoria sandwich cakes (page 14) | |
| | FILLING | |
| 100g/4 oz | unsalted butter, softened | 1 stick |
| 100g/4 oz | caster (fine) sugar | ½ cup |
| | 2 eggs, beaten | |
| 1 × 15ml spoon/ 1 tablespoon | coffee essence (strong black coffee) | 1 tablespoon |
| 3 × 15ml spoons/ 3 tablespoons | brandy | 4 tablespoons |
| | TOPPING | |
| 100g/4 oz | unsalted butter, softened | 1 stick |
| 175g/6 oz | icing (confectioner's) sugar, sifted | 1½ cups |
| 2 × 5ml spoons/ 2 teaspoons | instant coffee powder | 3 teaspoons |
| 50g/2 oz | chopped walnuts | ½ cup |

To make the filling, cream the butter until light and creamy, then beat in the sugar until fluffy. Gradually beat in the eggs, then the coffee essence and brandy.

Split each cake into three layers. Place one layer in a deep 17.5cm/7 inch cake tin (pan). Spoon over one-fifth of the filling, top with another layer of cake, and press down well. Continue making layers, ending with a cake layer. Weight down with a small plate, then chill for 4 hours.

Dip a knife in hot water, run it round the edge of the gâteau and turn out on to a plate.

To make the topping, beat the butter until creamy, then beat in the icing (confectioner's) sugar and coffee powder. Spread part over the gâteau, and pipe the rest on top. Decorate with chopped walnuts. Leave to set.

# MOCHA MERINGUE TORTE

| Metric/imperial | | American |
|---|---|---|
| 225g/8 oz | walnut halves | 2 cups |
| 175g/6 oz | icing (confectioner's) sugar, sifted | 1½ cups |
| | 3 egg whites | |
| | FILLING AND DECORATION | |
| 100g/4 oz | unsalted butter | 1 stick |
| 175g/6 oz | icing (confectioner's) sugar, sifted | 1½ cups |
| 2 × 15ml spoons/ 2 tablespoons | coffee essence (strong black coffee) | 3 tablespoons |
| | 2 egg yolks | |

Cut out two 20cm/8 inch circles from non-stick silicone paper. Place on a baking sheet.

Reserve a few walnut halves for decoration and grind the remainder finely in a blender or food processor. Alternatively, chop them very finely. Mix the ground walnuts with the icing sugar.

Whisk the egg whites until they form stiff peaks, then fold in the walnut mixture. Cover the greaseproof circles with the walnut meringue, dividing it equally between them.

Bake in a moderate oven, 180°C/350°F/Gas 4, for 35 minutes until the meringue is firm and crisp. Leave to cool, then carefully remove the paper.

To make the filling, cream the butter with the icing (confectioner's) sugar until light and fluffy, then work in the coffee essence. Beat in the egg yolks, one at a time.

Just before serving, sandwich the meringue rounds together with two-thirds of the buttercream, and use the remainder to pipe on the top. Decorate with the reserved walnut halves.

*Coffee Gâteau* **and** *Mocha Meringue Torte*

# MISSION SQUARES

*Makes 12*

| Metric/imperial | | American |
|---|---|---|
| 350g/12 oz | plain (all purpose) flour, sifted | 3 cups |
| 150g/5 oz | butter **or** margarine, diced | 1¼ sticks |
| 250g/9 oz | soft light brown sugar | 1⅓ cups, packed |
| 3 × 5ml spoons/ 3 teaspoons | baking powder | 4 teaspoons |
| | a pinch of salt | |
| | finely grated rind and juice of 1 orange | |
| 150g/5 oz | seedless raisins, finely chopped | scant 1 cup |
| 40g/1½ oz | shelled walnuts, finely chopped | scant ½ cup |
| | 2 eggs, beaten | |
| 6 × 15ml spoons/ 6 tablespoons | milk | 7 tablespoons |

Grease a 20cm/8 inch square cake tin (pan). Place the flour in a mixing bowl, add the fat and rub in with the fingertips until the mixture resembles fine breadcrumbs. Stir in the sugar. Press 225g/8 oz/½ US lb of the mixture into the prepared tin.

Stir the baking powder with the salt into the remaining rubbed-in mixture. Stir in the orange rind, raisins and walnuts. Beat the eggs with the orange juice and milk, then stir into the mixture. Beat well, then turn into the tin and level the surface.

Bake in a fairly hot oven, 190°C/375°F/Gas 5, for 1 hour until firm. Leave to cool in the tin (pan) for a few minutes, then turn out and cool completely. Cut into squares.

# MADELEINES

*Makes 18*

| Metric/imperial | | American |
|---|---|---|
| 115g/4½ oz | unsalted butter | 9 tablespoons |
| 100g/4 oz | caster (fine) sugar | ½ cup |
| | 2 eggs, beaten | |
| 100g/4 oz | plain (all purpose) flour | 1 cup |
| 1 × 5ml spoon/ 1 teaspoon | baking powder | 1 teaspoon |
| 1 × 5ml spoon/ 1 teaspoon | finely grated orange rind | 1 teaspoon |
| 1 × 15ml spoon/ 1 tablespoon | orange juice | 1 tablespoon |
| | **DECORATION** | |
| 1 × 15ml spoon/ 1 tablespoon | icing (confectioner's) sugar, sifted | 1 tablespoon |

Grease 18 shell-shaped madeleine tins (pans). Cream together the butter and sugar until light, fluffy and pale. Gradually beat in the eggs. Sift the flour with the baking powder, and fold into the creamed mixture with the orange rind and juice. Fill the prepared madeleine tins (pans) three-quarters full with the mixture.

Bake in a fairly hot oven, 200°C/400°F/Gas 6, for 8 minutes until risen and golden. Turn out on to a wire rack, and leave to cool.

When cold, sprinkle lightly with the icing (confectioner's) sugar.

**Note** These are the true French madeleines, not the sticky coconut castles which have adopted the name.

# CHOCOLATE CUP CAKES

*Makes 24*

| Metric/imperial | | American |
|---|---|---|
| 100g/4 oz | soft margarine | ¼ lb |
| 100g/4 oz | caster (fine) sugar | ½ cup |
| | 2 eggs, beaten | |
| 100g/4 oz | self-raising (self-rising) flour | 1 cup |
| 15g/½ oz | cocoa powder | 3 tablespoons |
| 1 × 5ml spoon/ 1 teaspoon | baking powder | 1 teaspoon |
| 175g/6 oz | TOPPING plain (semi-sweet) chocolate, broken into pieces | ⅓ lb |
| 20g/¾ oz | unsalted butter, diced | 1½ tablespoons |
| 175g/6 oz | icing (confectioner's) sugar, sifted | 1½ cups |
| 3 × 15ml spoons/ 3 tablespoons | warm water | 4 tablespoons |

Place 24 paper cake cases (paper baking cups) on a baking sheet. Cream together the margarine and sugar until light, fluffy and pale. Gradually beat in the eggs. Sift the flour with the cocoa and baking powder, and fold into the mixture. Beat well. Spoon the mixture into the paper cases (cups).

Bake in a fairly hot oven, 190°C/375°F/Gas 5, for 20 minutes until well risen and the tops spring back when pressed lightly. Transfer to a wire rack, and leave to cool.

To make the topping, place the chocolate and butter in a bowl set over a saucepan of gently simmering water, and heat until melted. Remove from the heat and beat in the icing (confectioner's) sugar and water. Beat until thick. Spoon on to the top of each cup cake, and leave until set.

# PEPPERMINT CREAM SLICES

*Makes about 12*

| Metric/imperial | | American |
|---|---|---|
| 225g/8 oz | self-raising (self-rising) flour | 2 cups |
| 2 × 5ml spoons/ 2 teaspoons | cocoa powder | 3 teaspoons |
| 100g/4 oz | soft light brown sugar | scant 1 cup, unpacked |
| 225g/8 oz | butter **or** margarine | 2 sticks |
| 225g/8 oz | TOPPING icing (confectioner's) sugar, sifted | 2 cups |
| | a few drops peppermint flavouring | |
| 175g/6 oz | plain (semi-sweet) chocolate, broken into pieces | ⅓ lb |

Grease a 32.5 × 17.5cm/13 × 9 inch Swiss roll tin (jelly roll pan). Sift the flour with the cocoa powder. Cream the sugar and fat in a mixing bowl until light and fluffy. Gradually beat in the flour mixture until well blended. Spread the mixture out in the prepared Swiss roll tin (jelly roll pan), and level the surface.

Bake in a fairly hot oven, 190°C/375°F/Gas 5, for 20 minutes until set. Leave to cool in the tin.

To make the topping, place the icing (confectioner's) sugar in a mixing bowl, and add just enough hot water to make a thick paste. Flavour to taste with peppermint flavouring. Spread over the chocolate biscuit.

Melt the chocolate in a bowl set over a saucepan of gently simmering water, then spread over the peppermint icing. Leave until cold, then cut into squares, and remove from the tin (pan).

# LEMON SQUARES

*Makes 20*

| Metric/imperial | | American |
|---|---|---|
| 175g/6 oz | butter | 1½ sticks |
| 175g/6 oz | caster (fine) sugar | scant 1 cup |
| | 2 eggs, beaten | |
| 175g/6 oz | self-raising (self-rising) flour, sifted | 1½ cups |
| | GLAZE | |
| | juice of 1 lemon | |
| 100g/4 oz | caster (fine) sugar | ½ cup |

Grease and base-line a 25 × 17.5cm/10 × 7 inch tin (pan). Cream together the butter and sugar until light, fluffy and pale. Gradually beat in the eggs, folding in a little of the flour after each addition. Fold in the remaining flour. Turn the mixture into the prepared tin (pan), and level the surface.

Bake in a moderate oven, 180°C/350°F/Gas 4, for 40 minutes until well risen and firm to the touch.

Meanwhile, mix together the lemon juice and sugar. As soon as the cake is removed from the oven, prick the top all over with a fork. Immediately pour over the lemon mixture, to cover the cake completely. Leave to cool in the tin (pan), then cut into squares.

**Note** The lemon juice sinks through to flavour the cake, and the sugar forms a crispy topping.

# COFFEE NUT MERINGUES

*Makes 6*

| Metric/imperial | | American |
|---|---|---|
| | 2 egg whites | |
| 100g/4 oz | caster (fine) sugar | ½ cup |
| ½ × 2.5ml spoon/ ¼ teaspoon | vinegar | ¼ teaspoon |
| 1 × 15ml spoon/ 1 tablespoon | coffee essence (strong black coffee) | 1 tablespoon |
| 1 × 5ml spoon/ 1 teaspoon | cornflour (cornstarch) | 1 teaspoon |
| 50g/2 oz | shelled walnuts, finely chopped | ½ cup |

Line a baking sheet with non-stick silicone paper. Whisk the egg whites until they form stiff peaks. Gradually whisk in the sugar until very stiff and glossy. Fold in the vinegar, coffee essence, cornflour (cornstarch) and walnuts. Using a teaspoon, place spoonfuls of the mixture on the prepared baking sheet.

Bake in a cool oven, 150°C/300°F/Gas 2, for 30 minutes until completely dry. Carefully remove the lining paper, transfer the meringues to a wire rack, and leave to cool. Serve plain.

# BROWN SUGAR MERINGUES

*Makes 6*

| Metric/imperial | | American |
|---|---|---|
| | 3 egg whites | |
| | a pinch of cream of tartar | |
| 175g/6 oz | soft light brown sugar | scant 1 cup, packed |
| 300ml/½ pint | double (heavy) cream, whipped | 1¼ cups |

Line a baking sheet with non-stick silicone paper. In a very clean, grease-free bowl, whisk the egg whites with the cream of tartar until they form stiff peaks. Whisk in half the sugar, then whisk in the remainder until very stiff and glossy. Using 2 tablespoons, place egg-shaped mounds of meringue on the prepared baking sheet.

Bake in a very cool oven, 120°C/250°F/Gas ½, for 1 hour until completely dry. Carefully remove the lining paper, transfer the meringues to a wire rack, and leave to cool.

When cold and just before serving, sandwich together with whipped cream.

### Variation
Add a little finely chopped stem ginger to the cream.

# MACAROONS

*Makes 18*

| Metric/imperial | | American |
|---|---|---|
| | 2 egg whites | |
| 225g/8 oz | caster (fine) sugar | 1 cup |
| 175g/6 oz | ground almonds | 1½ cups |
| | 18 blanched almonds | |

Line two ungreased baking trays with rice paper. Whisk the egg whites until they form stiff peaks, then fold in the sugar with the almonds. Spoon 18 small heaps of the mixture on to the prepared trays, leaving room for spreading. Top each with an almond.

Bake in a moderate oven, 180°C/350°/Gas 4, for 20 minutes until lightly browned. Leave to cool on the trays for 15 minutes, then carefully transfer to a wire rack. Leave to cool completely, then trim the rice paper round each macaroon.

# LITTLE HONEY CAKES

*Makes 16*

| Metric/imperial | | American |
|---|---|---|
| 450g/1 lb | clear honey | 1⅓ cups |
| 175g/6 oz | soft light brown sugar | scant 1 cup, packed |
| | 4 eggs, beaten | |
| 350g/12 oz | plain wholewheat flour | 3 cups |
| 1 × 5ml spoon/ 1 teaspoon | baking powder | 1 teaspoon |
| 1 × 5ml spoon/ 1 teaspoon | ground cinnamon | 1 teaspoon |
| ½ × 2.5ml spoon/ ¼ teaspoon | ground mixed spice | ¼ teaspoon |
| 50g/2 oz | sultanas (golden raisins) | ½ cup |
| 50g/2 oz | cut mixed peel (candied peel, chopped) | ½ cup |
| 50g/2 oz | blanched almonds, chopped | ½ cup |

Grease and line a 22.5cm/9 inch square tin (pan). Heat the honey and sugar in a saucepan over gentle heat, then leave to cool slightly. Beat in the eggs. Sift the flour with the baking powder and spices into a mixing bowl. Stir in the honey mixture, and beat until thoroughly combined, then stir in the sultanas (golden raisins), peel and almonds. Turn the mixture into the prepared tin (pan), and level the surface.

Bake in a fairly hot oven, 190°C/375°F/Gas 5, for 1 hour until golden-brown. Leave to cool in the tin (pan) for 10 minutes, then turn out on to a wire rack and leave to cool completely. Cut into squares.

# BRANDY SNAPS

*Makes 24*

| Metric/imperial | | American |
|---|---|---|
| 75g/3 oz | golden (light corn) syrup | ¼ cup |
| 40g/1½ oz | caster (fine) sugar | 4 tablespoons |
| 75g/3 oz | butter, diced | 6 tablespoons |
| 50g/2 oz | plain (all purpose) flour, sifted | ½ cup |
| 1 × 5ml spoon/ 1 teaspoon | ground ginger | 1 teaspoon |
| 1 × 5ml spoon/ 1 teaspoon | brandy | 1 teaspoon |
| | **FILLING** | |
| 150ml/¼ pint | double (heavy) cream, whipped | ⅝ cup |

Grease a baking sheet. Heat the syrup with the sugar and butter in a saucepan, over gentle heat, then leave to cool slightly. Stir in the flour and ginger, beat until smooth, then stir in the brandy. Using a teaspoon, place spoonfuls of the mixture on the prepared baking sheet, making sure they are well apart.

Bake in a moderate oven, 180°C/350°F/Gas 4, for 7 minutes until spread out and golden. Allow to cool slightly, but not to harden, then remove with a palette knife (metal spatula) and quickly roll each brandy snap round the greased handle of a wooden spoon. Slide off the spoon, and leave to cool and harden.

When cold, fill the brandy snaps with whipped cream.

*Brandy Snaps*

# COFFEE PORCUPINES

*Makes 15*

| Metric/imperial | | American |
|---|---|---|
| 150g/5 oz | self-raising (self-rising) flour | 1¼ cups |
| 1 × 5ml spoon/ 1 teaspoon | baking powder | 1 teaspoon |
| | 2 eggs, beaten | |
| 2 × 15ml spoons/ 2 tablespoons | coffee essence (strong black coffee) | 3 tablespoons |
| 100g/4 oz | soft margarine | ¼ lb |
| 100g/4 oz | caster (fine) sugar | ½ cup |

### TOPPING AND DECORATION

| | 1 recipe quantity Coffee Buttercream (page 74) | |
|---|---|---|
| 50g/2 oz | flaked (slivered) almonds, toasted | ½ cup |

Grease 15 bun tins (muffin pans). Sift the flour with the baking powder into a mixing bowl. Add the eggs, coffee essence, margarine and sugar, and beat vigorously for 2 minutes until smooth. Spoon the mixture into the prepared bun tins (muffin pans).

Bake in a fairly hot oven, 190°C/375°F/Gas 5, for 10 minutes until risen and golden. Turn out on to a wire rack, and leave to cool.

When cold, spread the cakes with Coffee Buttercream, and stick in toasted almonds to resemble porcupine quills.

**Note**   These cakes would be popular at a child's birthday party. For an even more realistic effect, use chocolate drops for the eyes.

# ICED FANCIES

*Makes about 16*

| Metric/imperial | | American |
|---|---|---|
| | 1 recipe quantity Genoese Sponge mixture (page 28) | |

### TOPPING AND DECORATION

| Metric/imperial | | American |
|---|---|---|
| 3 × 15ml spoons/ 3 tablespoons | apricot jam, warmed and sieved | 4 tablespoons |
| | 1 recipe quantity Almond Paste (page 74) | |
| | 1 recipe quantity Fondant Icing (page 76) | |
| | food colouring | |
| | small cake decorations | |

Bake the Genoese sponge mixture in a 20cm/8 inch square tin (pan). Turn out on to a wire rack, and leave to cool.

Cut the sponge into squares, rectangles or diamond shapes using a very sharp knife, then brush each cake with apricot jam to cover the top and sides.

Roll out the Almond Paste very thinly on a lightly floured surface, and cut into shapes to fit the top of each cake. Place a piece of Almond Paste on top of each cake. Cut strips of Almond Paste, and fit them neatly round the sides of each cake. Press the edges of the Almond Paste together firmly, and leave to set in a dry place for 12 hours.

Coat the cakes with Fondant Icing tinted in a variety of colourings. Decorate with small cake decorations such as silver dragées (balls), crystallized flower petals, mimosa balls, pieces of glacé (candied) cherry and angelica diamonds.

# ECCLES CAKES

*Makes 8*

| Metric/imperial | | American |
|---|---|---|
| 450g/1 lb | prepared shortcrust (basic pie) pastry | 1 lb |
| | FILLING AND GLAZE | |
| 100g/4 oz | currants | ¾ cup |
| 25g/1 oz | cut mixed peel (candied peel, chopped) | ¼ cup |
| 1 × 2.5ml spoon/ ½ teaspoon | ground allspice | ½ teaspoon |
| 1 × 2.5ml spoon/ ½ teaspoon | ground nutmeg | ½ teaspoon |
| 50g/2 oz | soft dark brown sugar | ½ cup, unpacked |
| 25g/1 oz | butter | 2 tablespoons |
| | 1 egg white | |
| 15g/½ oz | caster (fine) sugar | 1 tablespoon |

Roll out the pastry thinly on a lightly floured surface, then cut into 10cm/4 inch circles.

To make the filling, mix together the currants, peel and spices. Gently heat together the sugar and butter until melted, then stir in the fruit mixture. Allow to cool completely.

Using a teaspoon, place a heaped spoonful of the mixture in the centre of each pastry circle. Bring the edges together over the filling, and pinch together firmly to seal.

Turn the pastry parcels over, and place, seam side down, on a baking sheet. Brush with egg white, and sprinkle with the sugar.

Bake in a hot oven, 220°C/425°F/Gas 7, for 15 minutes until golden-brown. Using a fish slice, transfer to a wire rack, and leave to cool.

# PALMIERS

*Makes 8*

| Metric/imperial | | American |
|---|---|---|
| | sugar for sprinkling | |
| 225g/8 oz | prepared puff pastry | ½ lb |
| | FILLING | |
| 100g/4 oz | raspberry jam | 5 tablespoons |
| 300ml/½ pint | double (heavy) cream, whipped | 1¼ cups |

Dampen a baking sheet. Sprinkle a board with sugar. Roll out the pastry thinly to a large square on the sugared board. Trim the edges.

Sprinkle the pastry with more sugar, then roll lightly again. Fold the sides of the pastry to the centre, leaving a 1.25cm/ ½ inch gap down the middle. Sprinkle again with more sugar, and repeat the folding.

Turn one double fold directly over the other, and press firmly to form a rectangle. Cut crossways into 1.25cm/½ inch slices. Place on the prepared baking sheet, making sure they are well apart. Press down with the base of a jam jar, to flatten.

Bake in a hot oven, 220°C/425°F/Gas 7, for 8–10 minutes until golden. Turn over and bake for a further 3 minutes. Using a fish slice, transfer to a wire rack, and leave to cool.

When cold, sandwich together in pairs with jam and cream.

# RUM BABAS

*Makes 12*

| Metric/imperial | | American |
|---|---|---|
| | 1 recipe quantity Savarin dough, (page 35) unrisen | |
| 100g/4 oz | currants | $\frac{3}{4}$ cup |
| RUM SYRUP | | |
| 450g/1 lb | sugar | 2 cups |
| 450ml/$\frac{3}{4}$ pint | water | scant 2 cups |
| 3–4 × 15ml spoons/3–4 tablespoons | rum | 4–5 tablespoons |
| GLAZE AND DECORATION | | |
| 5 × 15ml spoons/ 5 tablespoons | apricot jam, warmed and sieved | 6 tablespoons |
| 150ml/$\frac{1}{4}$ pint | double (heavy) cream, whipped | $\frac{5}{8}$ cup |
| | 6 glacé (candied) cherries, halved | |

Prepare the dough as for the Savarin, adding the currants with the eggs and butter.

Half fill 12 greased dariole or castle pudding moulds with the dough. Stand them on a baking sheet and cover with clingfilm. Leave to prove in a warm place until the dough almost reaches the tops of the moulds (about 30–40 minutes).

Bake in a fairly hot oven, 200°C/400°F/Gas 6, for 15–20 minues until a deep golden-brown.

Meanwhile, make the rum syrup as in the Savarin recipe on page 35.

Remove the babas from the oven, and leave to cool in the moulds for 5 minutes, then turn out and trim the tops so that they stand upright. Place, cut side down, on a plate and prick well with a skewer. Pour over the rum syrup, and leave to cool.

Brush the babas with the apricot jam. Spoon or pipe the cream on top, and decorate each baba with a cherry half.

# BUTTERFLY CAKES

*Makes 15*

| Metric/imperial | | American |
|---|---|---|
| 150g/5 oz | self-raising (self-rising) flour | 1$\frac{1}{4}$ cups |
| 1 × 5ml spoon/ 1 teaspoon | baking powder | 1 teaspoon |
| | 2 eggs, beaten | |
| 100g/4 oz | soft margarine | $\frac{1}{4}$ lb |
| 100g/4 oz | caster (fine) sugar | $\frac{1}{2}$ cup |
| DECORATION Orange or Lemon Buttercream (page 74) | | |

Grease 15 bun tins (muffin pans). Sift the flour with the baking powder into a mixing bowl. Add the eggs, margarine and sugar, and beat vigorously for 2 minutes until smooth. Spoon the mixture into the prepared tins (muffin pans).

Bake in a fairly hot oven, 190°C/375°F/Gas 5 for 10 minutes until risen and the tops spring back when pressed lightly. Turn out on to a wire rack, and leave to cool.

When cold, cut a thin slice off the base of each cake and cut each slice in half. Spread the cut end of each cake with buttercream, and pipe a line of buttercream down the centre of each cake. Arrange the halved cake slices at an angle each side of the line of buttercream, to represent wings.

*Rum Babas*

# BISCUITS (COOKIES)

Home-made biscuits (cookies) are surprisingly quick, easy and inexpensive to make by a number of basic methods:

*Rolled biscuits (cookies):* a firm dough is rolled out thinly before being cut into shapes with a biscuit (cookie) or scone cutter, with the floured rim of a tumbler, or into fingers with a sharp knife.

*Piped biscuits (cookies):* are made from a firm dough which can be piped easily using a piping bag fitted with a large star or other nozzle.

*Tray biscuits (cookies):* shortbread and flapjack-type mixtures are pressed into a cake tin (pan) and pricked with a fork before baking. As soon as the baked mixture is taken from the oven, it should be marked into squares or fingers with a sharp knife, but only cut through when quite cold.

*Shaped biscuits (cookies):* biscuit (cookie) mixtures may be rolled into small balls with the hands, or spoonfuls placed on a baking sheet, with plenty of room to allow for spreading during baking. They should then be flattened slightly with a fork or palette knife (metal spatula) which has been dipped in water. Biscuit (cookie) dough may also be formed into a sausage shape or ball, and chilled or frozen before being cut into slices for baking.

Biscuits (cookies) should be baked on well-greased baking sheets or shallow tins unless the recipe states otherwise. They are usually baked at a moderate temperature for a short time, and care must be taken that they do not overbrown, which can happen very quickly. Do not judge whether they are done by their crispness: they will be soft when removed from the oven and will crisp up during cooling. They should be allowed to cool for a minute or two on the baking sheet before being carefully lifted on to a wire rack with a fish slice to cool completely. They should then be stored immediately in an airtight container.

## GIANT CURRANT COOKIES

*Makes about 15*

| Metric/imperial | | American |
|---|---|---|
| 100g/4 oz | self-raising (self-rising) flour | 1 cup |
| 100g/4 oz | fine semolina | $\frac{2}{3}$ cup |
| 100g/4 oz | butter, diced | 1 stick |
| 100g/4 oz | caster (fine) sugar | $\frac{1}{2}$ cup |
| | grated rind of 1 orange | |
| 100g/4 oz | currants | $\frac{3}{4}$ cup |
| | 2 eggs, beaten | |
| 1 × 15ml spoon/ 1 tablespoon | milk | 1 tablespoon |

Grease a baking sheet. Sift the flour with the semolina into a mixing bowl. Add the butter, and rub in with the fingertips until the mixture resembles fine breadcrumbs. Stir in the sugar, orange rind and currants. Add the eggs and milk, and mix to a stiff dough.

Turn on to a well floured surface and knead lightly, then roll out thinly. Cut out circles with a 7.5cm/3 inch fluted biscuit (cookie) cutter. Place on the prepared baking sheet.

Bake in a fairly hot oven, 190°C/375°F/Gas 5, for 12 minutes until golden-brown. Carefully transfer to a wire rack, and leave to cool.

# RAISIN SPICE COOKIES

*Makes about 20*

| Metric/imperial | | American |
|---|---|---|
| 100g/4 oz | self-raising (self-rising) flour | 1 cup |
| 1 × 2.5ml spoon/ ½ teaspoon | ground cinnamon | ½ teaspoon |
| ½ × 2.5ml spoon/ ¼ teaspoon | ground nutmeg | ¼ teaspoon |
| 100g/4 oz | fine semolina | ⅔ cup |
| 100g/4 oz | butter, diced | 1 stick |
| 100g/4 oz | caster (fine) sugar | ½ cup |
| | 2 eggs, beaten | |
| 1 × 15ml spoon/ 1 tablespoon | milk | 1 tablespoon |
| 75g/3 oz | seedless raisins | ½ cup |

Grease a baking sheet. Sift the flour with the spices and semolina into a mixing bowl. Rub in the butter. Stir in the sugar, then the eggs and milk, and finally the raisins, to make a stiff dough.

Turn on to a well floured surface, and knead lightly, then roll out thinly. Cut out circles with a 5cm/2 inch biscuit (cookie) cutter. Place on the prepared baking sheet.

Bake in a fairly hot oven, 190°C/375°F/Gas 5, for 12 minutes until golden. Carefully transfer to a wire rack, and leave to cool.

# FAIRINGS

*Makes about 20*

| Metric/imperial | | American |
|---|---|---|
| 150g/5 oz | self-raising (self-rising) flour | 1¼ cups |
| 100g/4 oz | fine semolina | ⅔ cup |
| ½ × 2.5ml spoon/ ¼ teaspoon | ground cinnamon | ¼ teaspoon |
| ½ × 2.5ml spoon/ ¼ teaspoon | ground ginger | ¼ teaspoon |
| 100g/4 oz | caster (fine) sugar | ½ cup |
| 100g/4 oz | butter, diced | 1 stick |
| | 1 egg, beaten | |
| | DECORATION | |
| 1 × 15ml spoon/ 1 tablespoon | caster (fine) sugar | 1 tablespoon |

Grease a baking sheet. Sift the flour with the semolina and spices into a mixing bowl, and stir in the sugar. Add the butter, and rub in with the fingertips until the mixture resembles coarse breadcrumbs. Work in the egg, and knead lightly until smooth.

Roll out thinly on a lightly floured surface, and cut out circles with a 5cm/2 inch biscuit (cookie) cutter. Place on the prepared baking sheet, and sprinkle with the caster (fine) sugar.

Bake in a moderate oven, 180°C/350°F/Gas 4, for 15 minutes until golden. Carefully transfer to a wire rack, and leave to cool.

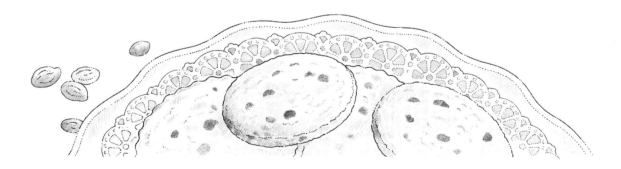

# Easter Biscuits (Cookies)

*Makes about 20*

| Metric/imperial | | American |
|---|---|---|
| 175g/6 oz | butter | 1½ sticks |
| 175g/6 oz | sugar | scant 1 cup |
| | 1 egg, beaten | |
| 350g/12 oz | plain (all purpose) flour | 3 cups |
| | a pinch of salt | |
| | a pinch of ground mixed spice | |
| 75g/3 oz | currants | ½ cup |
| 25g/1 oz | cut mixed peel (candied peel, chopped) | ¼ cup |
| | **GLAZE** 1 egg white, lightly beaten | |
| 1 × 15ml spoon/ 1 tablespoon | caster (fine) sugar | 1 tablespoon |

Grease a baking sheet. Cream together the butter and sugar, and work in the egg. Sift the flour with the salt and spice, and work into the mixture together with the currants and peel to make a fairly soft dough.

Turn on to a well floured surface, and knead lightly, then roll out thinly. Cut out circles with a 7.5cm/3 inch fluted biscuit (cookie) cutter. Place on the prepared baking sheet.

Bake in a moderate oven, 180°C/350°F/Gas 4, for 10 minutes until golden-brown.

Brush the biscuits (cookies) with the egg white, and sprinkle with the sugar. Return to the oven for 3 minutes. Carefully transfer to a wire rack, and leave to cool.

# Iced Lemon Biscuits (Cookies)

*Makes about 36*

| Metric/imperial | | American |
|---|---|---|
| 100g/4 oz | butter | 1 stick |
| 75g/3 oz | caster (fine) sugar | scant ½ cup |
| | 1 egg | |
| 1 × 5ml spoon/ 1 teaspoon | lemon juice | 1 teaspoon |
| 225g/8 oz | plain (all purpose) flour, sifted | 2 cups |
| | **ICING AND DECORATION** | |
| 100g/4 oz | icing (confectioner's) sugar, sifted | 1 cup |
| 2 × 5ml spoons/ 2 teaspoons | lemon juice | 3 teaspoons |
| | strips candied lemon peel | |

Grease a baking sheet. Cream together the butter and sugar, and work in the egg, lemon juice and flour. Knead to a soft dough, shape into a ball, wrap in clingfilm and chill for 30 minutes.

Roll out thinly on a lightly floured surface, and cut out circles with a 5cm/2 inch plain biscuit (cookie) cutter. Place on the prepared baking sheet.

Bake in a fairly hot oven, 190°C/375°F/Gas 5, for 10 minutes until golden. Carefully transfer to a wire rack, and leave to cool.

To make the icing, mix the icing (confectioner's) sugar with the lemon juice until smooth. Spread over the biscuits (cookies), and top with strips of candied lemon peel. Leave to set.

*Easter Biscuits*

# DUTCH SPECULAAS

*Makes about 36*

| Metric/imperial | | American |
|---|---|---|
| 75g/3 oz | butter | 6 tablespoons |
| 65g/2½ oz | soft light brown sugar | ½ cup, unpacked |
| 115g/4½ oz | self-raising (self-rising) flour | 1¼ cups |
| | a pinch of salt | |
| ½ × 2.5ml spoon/ ¼ teaspoon | ground mixed spice | ¼ teaspoon |
| ½ × 2.5ml spoon/ ¼ teaspoon | ground cinnamon | ¼ teaspoon |
| | grated rind of ½ lemon | |
| 50g/2 oz | blanched almonds, chopped | ½ cup |
| 15g/½ oz | digestive biscuits (Graham crackers), crushed | 2 tablespoons |
| | **DECORATION** | |
| 1 × 15ml spoon/ 1 tablespoon | icing (confectioner's) sugar, sifted | 1 tablespoon |

Grease a baking sheet. Cream together the butter and sugar until light and fluffy. Sift the flour with the salt and spices, and work into the creamed mixture with the lemon rind, almonds and biscuit crumbs.

Knead well, then roll out thinly on a lightly floured surface. Cut out heart, animal or Christmas tree shapes. Place on the prepared baking sheet.

Bake in a moderate oven, 180°C/350°F/Gas 4, for 10–15 minutes until golden-brown. Carefully transfer to a wire rack, and leave to cool. Sprinkle lightly with icing (confectioner's) sugar.

# DUTCH KERSTKRANSJES

*Makes about 36*

| Metric/imperial | | American |
|---|---|---|
| 100g/4 oz | butter | 1 stick |
| 1 × 5ml spoon/ 1 teaspoon | vanilla flavouring | 1 teaspoon |
| 150g/5 oz | plain (all purpose) flour | 1¼ cups |
| 50g/2 oz | icing (confectioner's) sugar | ½ cup |
| | a pinch of salt | |
| | 1 egg, beaten | |
| | **GLAZE** 1 egg, beaten | |
| 25g/1 oz | blanched almonds, finely chopped | ¼ cup |
| 25g/1 oz | sugar | 3 tablespoons |

Cream the butter with the vanilla flavouring until light and creamy. Sift the flour with the icing (confectioner's) sugar and salt, and work into the butter. Knead thoroughly until smooth, then work in sufficient egg to bind. Shape into a ball, wrap in clingfilm and chill for 1 hour.

Roll out thinly on a lightly floured surface. Cut out circles with a 6.25cm/2½ inch plain cutter, and cut out the centres with a 2.5cm/1 inch cutter. Re-roll the trimmings, and repeat.

Brush the rings with egg, and sprinkle with the almonds and sugar. Place on an ungreased baking sheet, and bake in a moderate oven, 180°C/350°F/Gas 4, for 10–15 minutes until golden-brown. Carefully transfer to a wire rack, and leave to cool.

# ORANGE CRESCENTS

*Makes about 24*

| Metric/imperial | | American |
|---|---|---|
| 150g/5 oz | plain (all purpose) flour, sifted | 1¼ cups |
| 50g/2 oz | fine semolina | ⅓ cup |
| 75g/3 oz | butter, diced | 6 tablespoons |
| 50g/2 oz | caster (fine) sugar | ¼ cup |
| 1 × 5ml spoon/ 1 teaspoon | finely grated orange rind | 1 teaspoon |
| | 1 egg yolk | |
| 2 × 5ml spoons/ 2 teaspoons | cold water | 3 teaspoons |
| | GLAZE 1 egg white, lightly beaten | |
| 2 × 5ml spoons/ 2 teaspoons | caster (fine) sugar | 3 teaspoons |

Grease a baking sheet. Combine the flour and semolina in a mixing bowl, add the butter and rub in with the fingertips until the mixture resembles fine breadcrumbs. Add the sugar and orange rind, and mix to a stiff dough with the egg yolk beaten with the water.

Turn on to a lightly floured surface and knead until smooth, then roll out thinly. Cut into crescent shapes and place on the prepared baking sheet. Brush with the egg white, then sprinkle with the sugar.

Bake in a moderate oven, 180°C/350°F/Gas 4, for 10 minutes until light golden. Carefully transfer to a wire rack, and leave to cool.

# OATMEAL TEA BISCUITS (COOKIES)

*Makes about 40*

| Metric/imperial | | American |
|---|---|---|
| 225g/8 oz | fine oatmeal | 2⅔ cups |
| 225g/8 oz | plain wholewheat flour | 2 cups |
| | a pinch of salt | |
| 100g/4 oz | butter **or** margarine, diced | 1 stick |
| 100g/4 oz | soft light brown sugar | scant 1 cup, unpacked |
| ½ × 2.5ml spoon/ ¼ teaspoon | ground cinnamon | ¼ teaspoon |
| 1 × 5ml spoon/ 1 teaspoon | cream of tartar | 1 teaspoon |
| 1 × 1.25ml spoon/ ¼ teaspoon | bicarbonate of soda (baking soda) | ¼ teaspoon |
| | 1 egg, beaten | |
| | milk | |

Grease a baking sheet. Combine the oatmeal, flour and salt in a mixing bowl. Add the fat, and rub in with the fingertips until the mixture resembles fine breadcrumbs. Stir in the sugar, cinnamon, cream of tartar and soda. Mix to a fairly soft dough with the egg and a little milk.

Turn on to a lightly floured surface, and knead until smooth, then roll out thinly. Cut out 5cm/2 inch rounds with a fluted biscuit (cookie) cutter. Place on the prepared baking sheet, and prick with a fork.

Bake in a hot oven, 180°C/350°F/Gas 4, for 15 minutes until golden. Carefully transfer to a wire rack, and leave to cool.

**Note** These biscuits (cookies) are good as a sweet biscuit (cookie), but are also delicious with cheese.

# SAVOURY DIGESTIVE BISCUITS (GRAHAM CRACKERS)

*Makes 50*

| Metric/imperial | | American |
|---|---|---|
| 225g/8 oz | plain wholewheat flour | 2 cups |
| 100g/4 oz | plain (all purpose) white flour | 1 cup |
| 1 × 2.5ml spoon/ ½ teaspoon | salt | ½ teaspoon |
| 75g/3 oz | hard margarine, diced | 6 tablespoons |
| 50g/2 oz | lard (shortening), diced | 4 tablespoons |
| | 1 egg | |
| 4 × 15ml spoons/ 4 tablespoons | water | 5 tablespoons |
| 2 × 5ml spoons/ 2 teaspoons | yeast (vegetable) extract | 3 teaspoons |

Grease two baking sheets. Sift the flours with the salt into a mixing bowl. Add the fats, and rub in with the fingertips until the mixture resembles fine breadcrumbs. Beat the egg with the water and stir in the yeast (vegetable) extract. Add to the mixture, and mix well to give a soft dough.

Roll out the dough thinly on a lightly floured surface, and cut out 5cm/2 inch rounds with a plain cutter. Transfer with a fork.

Bake in a moderate oven, 180°C/350°F/Gas 4, for 15 minutes until lightly browned. Carefully transfer to a wire rack, and leave to cool.

# WHOLEWHEAT CHEESE BISCUITS (COOKIES)

*Makes about 30*

| Metric/imperial | | American |
|---|---|---|
| 100g/4 oz | plain wholewheat flour | 1 cup |
| ½ × 2.5ml spoon/ ¼ teaspoon | salt | ¼ teaspoon |
| 1 × 5ml spoon/ 1 teaspoon | mustard powder | 1 teaspoon |
| 25g/1 oz | butter **or** margarine, diced | 2 tablespoons |
| 225g/8 oz | Cheddar (hard) cheese, finely grated | ½ lb |
| 2 × 15ml spoons/ 2 tablespoons | cold water | 3 tablespoons |

Grease a baking sheet. Sift the flour with the salt and mustard into a mixing bowl. Add the fat, and rub in with the fingertips until the mixture resembles fine breadcrumbs. Add the grated cheese, and mix to a dough with the water.

Turn on to a lightly floured surface, and knead until smooth, then roll out thinly. Cut out 5cm/2 inch rounds with a plain biscuit (cookie) cutter. Place on the prepared baking sheet, and prick with a fork.

Bake in a very hot oven, 230°C/450°F/Gas 8, for 7 minutes until puffed and lightly browned. Carefully transfer to a wire rack, and leave to cool.

*Wholewheat Cheese Biscuits (Cookies)* **and** *Savoury Digestive Biscuits (Graham Crackers)*

# Nut Shortbread Fingers

*Makes about 30*

| Metric/imperial | | American |
|---|---|---|
| 300g/10 oz | plain (all purpose) flour, sifted | 2½ cups |
| 75g/3 oz | caster (fine) sugar | scant ½ cup |
| 225g/8 oz | butter, diced | 2 sticks |
| | a few drops vanilla flavouring | |
| 50g/2 oz | hazelnuts, finely chopped | ½ cup |
| 25g/1 oz | candied angelica, chopped | 2 tablespoons |

Lightly grease a baking sheet. Combine the flour and sugar in a large mixing bowl. Add the butter, and rub in with the fingertips until the mixture resembles coarse breadcrumbs. Stir in the vanilla flavouring, nuts and angelica. Knead lightly until smooth.

Roll out on a lightly floured surface to 6mm/¼ inch thickness and cut into 7.5 × 2.5cm/3 × 1 inch fingers. Place on the prepared baking sheet, and chill for 10 minutes.

Bake in a fairly hot oven, 190°C/375°F/Gas 5, for 10 minutes until golden. Carefully transfer to a wire rack, and leave to cool.

# Viennese Biscuits (Cookies)

*Makes about 24*

| Metric/imperial | | American |
|---|---|---|
| 175g/6 oz | butter **or** margarine | 1½ sticks |
| 40g/1½ oz | icing (confectioner's) sugar, sifted | scant ½ cup |
| | a few drops vanilla flavouring | |
| 115g/4½ oz | plain (all purpose) flour | 1¼ cups |
| 40g/1½ oz | cornflour (cornstarch) | scant ½ cup |

DECORATION
glacé (candied)
cherries, quartered

Grease a baking sheet. Cream together the fat and icing (confectioner's) sugar until light, fluffy and pale. Beat in the vanilla flavouring. Sift the flour with the cornflour (cornstarch), and fold into the creamed mixture.

Place the mixture in a piping bag fitted with a star nozzle, and pipe stars on to the prepared baking sheet. Place a piece of cherry in the centre of each star.

Bake in a moderate oven, 180°C/350°F/Gas 4, for 15–20 minutes until light golden. Carefully transfer to a wire rack, and leave to cool.

# DANISH VANILLA WREATHS

*Makes about 40*

| Metric/imperial | | American |
|---|---|---|
| 250g/9 oz | plain (all purpose) flour, sifted | 2¼ cups |
| ½ × 2.5ml spoon/ ¼ teaspoon | baking powder | ¼ teaspoon |
| 175g/6 oz | butter, softened | 1½ sticks |
| 115g/4½ oz | sugar | generous ½ cup |
| 50g/2 oz | ground almonds | ½ cup |
| | 2 drops vanilla flavouring | |
| | 1 egg, beaten | |

Grease a baking sheet. Place all the ingredients in a mixing bowl, and beat well until thoroughly combined. Allow to stand in a cool place for 20 minutes.

Place the mixture in a piping bag fitted with a medium star vegetable nozzle, and pipe small rings on to the prepared baking sheet. (Add a little milk if the mixture is too stiff.)

Bake in a fairly hot oven, 200°C/400°F/Gas 6, for 10 minutes until golden. Carefully transfer to a wire rack, and leave to cool.

# CHOCOLATE SHORTBREAD

*Makes about 15 pieces*

| Metric/imperial | | American |
|---|---|---|
| 225g/8 oz | butter | 2 sticks |
| 75g/3 oz | icing (confectioner's) sugar, sifted | ¾ cup |
| 250g/9 oz | plain (all purpose) flour, sifted | 2¼ cups |
| 25g/1 oz | cocoa powder | ¼ cup |
| 50g/2 oz | flaked (slivered) almonds | ½ cup |

Grease a 17.5cm × 27.5cm/7 × 11 inch tin (pan). Cream together the butter and sugar, and work in the flour and cocoa until the mixture is smooth and thoroughly combined. Press into the prepared tin (pan), prick with a fork and sprinkle the almonds evenly over the top.

Bake in a warm oven, 160°C/325°F/Gas 3, for 40 minutes until firm. Mark into fingers with a sharp knife, then leave to cool in the tin (pan). Cut into fingers.

# GINGER SHORTCAKE

*Makes about 8 pieces*

| Metric/imperial | | American |
|---|---|---|
| 175g/6 oz | plain (all purpose) flour | 1½ cups |
| | a pinch of salt | |
| 1 × 2.5ml/ ½ teaspoon | ground ginger | ½ teaspoon |
| 100g/4 oz | butter, diced | 1 stick |
| 50g/2 oz | caster (fine) sugar | ¼ cup |
| | **ICING** | |
| 50g/2 oz | unsalted butter | 4 tablespoons |
| 25g/1 oz | icing (confectioner's) sugar, sifted | ¼ cup |
| 1 × 5ml spoon/ 1 teaspoon | ground ginger | 1 teaspoon |
| 1 × 15ml spoon/ 1 tablespoon | golden (light corn) syrup | 1 tablespoon |

Grease and base-line a 20cm/8 inch sandwich tin (layer pan). Sift the flour with the salt and ginger into a mixing bowl. Add the butter, and rub in with the fingertips until the mixture resembles fine breadcrumbs. Stir in the sugar, and knead to a smooth dough.

Turn the dough on to a lightly floured surface, and roll out to a round 1.25cm/½ inch thick that will fit into the prepared tin. Place in the tin, and crimp the edges. Prick lightly all over with a fork.

Bake in a cool oven, 150°C/300°F/Gas 2, for 45 minutes until golden. Turn out on to a wire rack, and mark into triangles with a sharp knife.

To make the icing, place all the ingredients in a heavy-based saucepan, and heat gently until melted. Beat well. Pour over the warm shortbread, then leave until cold. Cut into triangles.

# ALMOND SHORTBREAD

*Makes about 18 pieces*

| Metric/imperial | | American |
|---|---|---|
| 200g/7 oz | plain (all purpose) flour | 1¾ cups |
| 25g/1 oz | ground rice | ¼ cup |
| 25g/1 oz | blanched almonds, chopped | ¼ cup |
| 75g/3 oz | caster (fine) sugar | scant ½ cup |
| 25g/1 oz | cut mixed peel (candied peel, chopped) | ¼ cup |
| 175g/6 oz | butter, softened | 1½ sticks |

Grease a 33.5 × 22.5cm/13 × 9 inch Swiss roll tin (jelly roll pan). Sift the flour with the rice into a mixing bowl. Stir in the almonds, sugar and peel. Add the butter and rub in with the fingertips until the mixture resembles coarse breadcrumbs. Knead well to make a soft dough. Press into the prepared tin (pan), then prick lightly all over with a fork.

Bake in a very cool oven, 140°C/275°F/Gas 1, for 1 hour until golden. Mark into squares with a sharp knife, then leave to cool in the tin (pan). Cut into squares.

*Ginger Shortcake, Melting Shortbread (page 66), Chocolate Shortbread (page 63)* **and** *Almond Shortbread*

# MELTING SHORTBREAD

*Makes about 15 pieces*

| Metric/imperial | | American |
|---|---|---|
| 225g/8 oz | butter | 2 sticks |
| 100g/4 oz | icing (confectioner's) sugar, sifted | 1 cup |
| 225g/8 oz | plain (all purpose) flour, sifted | 2 cups |
| 100g/4 oz | cornflour (cornstarch) | 1 cup |
| | a pinch of salt | |
| | DECORATION | |
| 1 × 15ml spoon/ 1 tablespoon | caster (fine) sugar | 1 tablespoon |

Cream together the butter and sugar until light, fluffy and pale. Sift the flour with the cornflour (cornstarch) and salt, and work into the creamed mixture to make a smooth dough. Press into an ungreased 17.5 × 27.5cm/7 × 11 inch shallow tin (pan), and prick with a fork.

Bake in a warm oven, 160°C/325°F/Gas 3, for 40 minutes until light golden. Sprinkle with caster (fine) sugar, then mark into squares with a sharp knife, and leave to cool in the tin (pan). Cut into squares.

# CHOCOLATE FRUIT FLAPJACKS

*Makes about 9*

| Metric/imperial | | American |
|---|---|---|
| 75g/3 oz | butter **or** margarine | 6 tablespoons |
| 2 × 15ml spoons/ 2 tablespoons | golden (light corn) syrup | 3 tablespoons |
| 100g/4 oz | porridge oats | 1⅓ cups |
| 25g/1 oz | Demerara (brown) sugar | 3 tablespoons |
| 25g/1 oz | cut mixed peel (candied peel, chopped) | ¼ cup |
| 25g/1 oz | glacé (candied) cherries, rinsed, dried and quartered | 3 tablespoons |
| 25g/1 oz | shelled walnuts, chopped | ¼ cup |
| | TOPPING | |
| 50g/2 oz | plain (semi-sweet) chocolate, broken into pieces | ½ cup |
| 1 × 15ml spoon/ 1 tablespoon | unsalted butter **or** margarine | 1 tablespoon |

Grease and line a 17.5cm/7 inch square shallow tin (pan). Melt the fat and syrup in a saucepan over gentle heat. Stir in the oats, sugar, peel, cherries and walnuts. Press the mixture into the prepared tin (pan), and prick with a fork.

Bake in a moderate oven, 180°C/350°F/Gas 4, for 25 minutes until firm. Leave to cool in the tin (pan) for 15 minutes, then turn out on to a wire rack, and leave to cool completely.

To make the topping, melt together the chocolate and fat in a bowl set over a saucepan of gently simmering water. Stir well and allow to cool slightly, then spread over the baked mixture and leave to set. Cut into fingers.

# Coconut Flapjacks

*Makes about 18*

| Metric/imperial | | American |
|---|---|---|
| 100g/4 oz | butter **or** margarine, melted | 1 stick |
| 150g/5 oz | self-raising (self-rising) flour, sifted | 1¼ cups |
| 150g/5 oz | sugar | scant ¾ cup |
| 25g/1 oz | cornflakes | 1 cup |
| 65g/2½ oz | desiccated (shredded) coconut | ¾ cup |

Grease a 22.5 × 30cm/9 × 12 inch tin (pan). Place all the ingredients in a mixing bowl, and beat well until thoroughly combined. Press the mixture into the prepared tin (pan), and prick with a fork.

Bake in a moderate oven, 180°C/350°F/Gas 4, for 30 minutes until golden. Cool for 5 minutes in the tin (pan), then mark into squares with a sharp knife. Leave to cool completely in the tin (pan), then cut into squares.

# Ginger Muesli Biscuits (Granola Cookies)

*Makes about 9*

| Metric/imperial | | American |
|---|---|---|
| 225g/8 oz | muesli (granola) | 2½ cups |
| 1 × 2.5ml spoon/ ½ teaspoon | ground ginger | ½ teaspoon |
| 100g/4 oz | butter **or** margarine | 1 stick |
| 2 × 15ml spoons/ 2 tablespoons | clear honey | 3 tablespoons |
| | 1 egg, beaten | |
| 25g/1 oz | plain (all purpose) flour, sifted | ¼ cup |

Grease a 17.5cm/7 inch square shallow tin (pan). Combine the muesli (granola) with the ginger in a mixing bowl. Melt the fat and honey in a saucepan over gentle heat. Cool slightly, then stir into the dry ingredients. Stir in the egg and flour, and mix well. Press into the prepared tin (pan), and prick with a fork.

Bake in a cool oven, 150°C/300°F/Gas 2, for 45 minutes. Cool slightly, then mark into squares with a sharp knife. Leave to cool completely, then cut into squares.

# COFFEE KISSES

*Makes about 12*

| Metric/imperial | | American |
|---|---|---|
| 175g/6 oz | self-raising (self-rising) flour | 1½ cups |
| | a pinch of salt | |
| 75g/3 oz | butter, diced | 6 tablespoons |
| 50g/2 oz | caster (fine) sugar | ¼ cup |
| 50g/2 oz | cornflakes | 2 cups |
| | 1 egg yolk | |
| 1 × 5ml spoon/ 1 teaspoon | coffee essence (strong black coffee) | 1 teaspoon |
| | milk | |
| | **FILLING** | |
| 25g/1 oz | unsalted butter | 2 tablespoons |
| 50g/2 oz | icing (confectioner's) sugar, sifted | ½ cup |
| 1 × 5ml spoon/ 1 teaspoon | coffee essence (strong black coffee) | 1 teaspoon |

Grease a baking sheet. Sift the flour with the salt into a mixing bowl. Add the butter, and rub in with the fingertips until the mixture resembles fine breadcrumbs. Stir in the sugar and cornflakes. Add the egg yolk and coffee essence, and mix to a soft dough with a little milk.

Divide the dough into 24 balls. Place on the prepared baking sheet making sure they are spaced well apart. Flatten slightly with a palette knife (metal spatula) dipped in water.

Bake in a fairly hot oven, 190°C/375°F/Gas 5, for about 15 minutes until golden. Transfer to a wire rack, and cool completely.

To make the filling, cream together the butter and icing sugar until light, fluffy and pale. Beat in the coffee essence. Use to sandwich the biscuits (cookies) together in pairs.

# JUMBLES

*Makes about 24*

| Metric/imperial | | American |
|---|---|---|
| 150g/5 oz | butter | 1¼ sticks |
| 150g/5 oz | caster (fine) sugar | scant ¾ cup |
| | 1 egg, beaten | |
| 275g/10 oz | plain (all purpose) flour, sifted | 2½ cups |
| 1 × 5ml spoon/ 1 teaspoon | finely grated lemon rind | 1 teaspoon |
| 50g/2 oz | ground almonds | ½ cup |

Grease a baking sheet. Cream together the butter and sugar until light, fluffy and pale. Work in the egg. Fold in the flour with the lemon rind and ground almonds. Knead lightly to make a soft dough.

Roll the dough into a narrow sausage shape. Cut off 3.5cm/ 1½ inch lengths and form each into an 'S' shape. Place on the prepared baking sheet.

Bake in a moderate oven, 180°C/350°F/Gas 4, for 10 minutes until golden. Carefully transfer to a wire rack, and leave to cool.

# GINGER SNAPS

*Makes about 24*

| Metric/imperial | | American |
|---|---|---|
| 225g/8 oz | plain (all purpose) flour | 2 cups |
| 100g/4 oz | soft dark brown sugar | scant 1 cup, unpacked |
| | a pinch of salt | |
| 1 × 2.5ml spoon/ ½ teaspoon | bicarbonate of soda (baking soda) | ½ teaspoon |
| 1 × 5ml spoon/ 1 teaspoon | ground ginger | 1 teaspoon |
| 40g/1½ oz | lard (shortening) | 3 tablespoons |
| 25g/1 oz | butter | 2 tablespoons |
| 100g/4 oz | golden (light corn) syrup | ⅓ cup |
| | 1 egg, beaten | |

Grease a baking sheet. Sift the flour with the sugar, salt, soda and ginger. Place the lard (shortening), butter and syrup in a heavy-based saucepan, and heat gently until melted. Cool slightly, then stir into the dry ingredients. Stir in the egg, shape into a ball, wrap in clingfilm, and chill for 1 hour.

Take walnut-sized pieces of the dough, roll out on a lightly floured surface, and place on the prepared baking sheet. Flatten with a fork.

Bake in a moderate oven, 180°C/350°F/Gas 4, for 10 minutes until firm. Carefully transfer to a wire rack, and leave to cool.

# HUNGARIAN CHOCOLATE BISCUITS (COOKIES)

*Makes about 15*

| Metric/imperial | | American |
|---|---|---|
| 225g/8 oz | butter | 2 sticks |
| 100g/4 oz | caster (fine) sugar | ½ cup |
| 225g/8 oz | self-raising (self-rising) flour, sifted | 2 cups |
| 50g/2 oz | cocoa powder | ½ cup |
| 1 × 5ml spoon/ 1 teaspoon | vanilla flavouring | 1 teaspoon |
| | **FILLING** | |
| 50g/2 oz | cocoa powder | ½ cup |
| 3 × 15ml spoons/ 3 tablespoons | strong coffee | 4 tablespoons |
| 50g/2 oz | unsalted butter | 4 tablespoons |
| 50g/2 oz | caster (fine) sugar | ¼ cup |

Grease a baking sheet. Cream together the butter and sugar. Work in the flour, cocoa and vanilla flavouring to make a soft dough. Take walnut-sized pieces of the dough, roll into balls and place on the prepared baking sheet, making sure they are spaced well apart. Flatten with a fork dipped in water.

Bake in a moderate oven, 180°C/350°F/Gas 4, for 12 minutes until firm. Carefully transfer to a wire rack, and leave to cool.

To make the filling, mix the cocoa and coffee to a paste, and heat gently in a small heavy-based saucepan. Remove from the heat, and beat in the butter, then the sugar, until thick and creamy. Leave until cold, then use to sandwich together the biscuits (cookies) in pairs.

# CHOCOLATE GINGERS

*Makes about 20*

| Metric/imperial | | American |
|---|---|---|
| 75g/3 oz | butter **or** margarine | 6 tablespoons |
| 75g/3 oz | golden (light corn) syrup | ¼ cup |
| 50g/2 oz | plain (all purpose) flour, sifted | ½ cup |
| 50g/2 oz | sugar | ¼ cup |
| 1 × 2.5ml spoon/ ½ teaspoon | ground ginger | ½ teaspoon |
| | TOPPING | |
| 100g/4 oz | cube sugar | ¼ lb |
| 25g/1 oz | blanched almonds, chopped | ¼ cup |
| 25g/1 oz | cut mixed peel (candied peel, chopped) | ¼ cup |
| 175g/6 oz | plain (semi-sweet) chocolate, broken into pieces | ⅓ lb |

Grease a baking sheet. Melt the fat and syrup in a saucepan over gentle heat. Cool slightly, then stir in the flour, sugar and ginger. Using a teaspoon, place spoonfuls of the mixture on the prepared baking sheet, making sure they are spaced well apart.

Bake in a moderate oven, 180°C/350°F/Gas 4, for 10 minutes until lightly browned. Carefully transfer to a wire rack, and leave to cool completely.

To make the topping, place the cube sugar in a heavy-based saucepan, and heat until melted and pale brown. Add the almonds and peel, stir well and quickly spread over the biscuits (cookies). Leave until set.

Meanwhile, melt the chocolate in a basin set over hot water. Turn the biscuits (cookies) over, and coat the flat sides with the melted chocolate. Mark in lines with a fork, and leave to set.

# CARAWAY BISCUITS (COOKIES)

*Makes about 36*

| Metric/imperial | | American |
|---|---|---|
| 100g/4 oz | butter | 1 stick |
| 200g/7 oz | sugar | scant 1 cup |
| | 1 egg, beaten | |
| 350g/12 oz | plain (all purpose) flour | 3 cups |
| ½ × 2.5ml spoon/ ¼ teaspoon | salt | ¼ teaspoon |
| | grated rind of 1 lemon | |
| 2 × 15ml spoons/ 2 tablespoons | lemon juice | 3 tablespoons |
| ½ × 2.5ml spoon/ ¼ teaspoon | bicarbonate of soda (baking soda) | ¼ teaspoon |
| 1½ × 5ml spoons/ 1½ teaspoons | caraway seeds | 2 teaspoons |

Grease a baking sheet. Cream together the butter and sugar until light, fluffy and pale. Work in the egg. Sift the flour with the salt, then fold into the mixture with the lemon rind and juice, soda and caraway seeds. Mix to a firm dough and roll into a sausage shape, about 5cm/2 inches thick. Cut into 1.25cm/ ½ inch slices. Place on the prepared baking sheet.

Bake in a fairly hot oven, 200°C/400°F/Gas 6, for 10 minutes until golden. Carefully transfer to a wire rack, and leave to cool.

# COFFEE OVALS

*Makes about 30*

| Metric/imperial | | American |
|---|---|---|
| 175g/6 oz | butter | 1½ sticks |
| 100g/4 oz | sugar | ½ cup |
| 2 × 15ml spoons/ 2 tablespoons | coffee essence (strong black coffee) | 3 tablespoons |
| 250g/9 oz | plain (all purpose) flour, sifted | 2¼ cups |
| 25g/1 oz | mixed nuts, chopped | ¼ cup |

Grease a baking sheet. Cream together the butter and sugar until light, fluffy and pale. Stir in the coffee essence, then work in the flour. Knead lightly until smooth, then divide the dough in half and roll each piece into a sausage shape. Roll each in the chopped nuts, then wrap in clingfilm and chill for 1 hour.

Slice each roll at an angle to make oval-shaped biscuits, and place on the prepared baking sheet.

Bake in a moderate oven, 180°C/350°F/Gas 4, for 15 minutes until light brown. Carefully transfer to a wire rack, and leave to cool.

# ALMOND TUILES

*Makes about 24*

| Metric/imperial | | American |
|---|---|---|
| 65g/2½ oz | butter | 5 tablespoons |
| 50g/2 oz | caster (fine) sugar | ¼ cup |
| 40g/1½ oz | plain (all purpose) flour, sifted | scant ½ cup |
| 40g/1½ oz | flaked (slivered) almonds | scant ½ cup |
| | 2 drops almond favouring | |

Grease a baking sheet. Cream together the butter and sugar until light, fluffy and pale. Fold in the flour, almonds and flavouring.

Form the mixture into marble-sized balls, and place six, 7.5cm/3 inches apart, on the prepared baking sheet. Flatten each ball with the back of a fork dipped in water.

Bake in a fairly hot oven, 200°C/400°F/Gas 6, for 8–10 minutes until light golden with brown edges. Remove from the oven, and leave to stand for just a few seconds to set.

Peel the tuiles off the tin with a very sharp knife, and lift carefully on to an oiled rolling-pin, to form a slight curve. Slide off the rolling-pin, and leave to harden, then store immediately in an airtight container. Repeat until all the tuiles are baked.

**Note** Do not attempt to bake more than six tuiles at à time, or they will harden on the baking sheet and be difficult to remove. Should this happen, return to the oven for a minute or two to soften.

# ICINGS

Many cakes benefit from some kind of icing or decorative topping, but it is very important to choose a suitable finish for individual cakes. For instance, a glacé icing is perfect for sponge cakes, but does not look or taste right with a rich fruit cake; on the other hand, the solid royal icing which traditionally tops a Christmas cake would be totally unsuitable for a light sponge cake. There are also a number of basic icings which may be varied by flavouring and colouring.

## Icing Equipment

The simplest forms of icing require a minimum of equipment. A nylon sieve is essential as a wire sieve will taint icing sugar. Otherwise, only a bowl and spoon are needed for mixing, plus a palette knife (metal spatula) for applying the icing. A turntable is useful if you do a lot of icing, as the cake can be placed on this and turned slowly so that the icing does not become smudged or uneven. Alternatively, you can improvize with a cake board which may be placed on an upturned bowl and easily rotated.

Cake decoration is a fascinating skill and you will want to acquire more sophisticated equipment as you progress, but for simple piping all you will require is a piping bag – the 30cm/ 12 inch size is most useful – and some basic piping nozzles: a writing tube and large and small star nozzles will give a sufficient variety of patterns to start off with.

## Basic Icings

*Glacé icing* is a blend of icing (confectioner's) sugar and water or other liquid, such as fruit juice, which spreads very easily and dries quickly. It is suitable for small cakes, light sponges and biscuits. As the icing cracks after a few days, it is best used on cakes which are going to be eaten quickly. Glacé icing makes biscuits soft, so is best spread on them shortly before serving. It also does not hold its shape, so is not used for pipings, although it may be thickened with extra sugar and used for writing.

*Buttercream* is a mixture of butter – unsalted gives best results – icing sugar and flavouring. Soft margarine gives a good texture, and may be substituted for butter, but is best combined with a strong flavouring such as chocolate or coffee. Buttercream may be used as a filling as well as a topping and is ideal for piping on sponges and gâteaux. It freezes well (see page 10).

*Almond paste* or marzipan is a mixture of ground almonds, sugar and egg. It is used under other icings – particularly royal icing and fondant – but may also be used alone to cover a cake, such as a rich fruit cake. It is always applied over a thin coating of jam to help it adhere and prevent cake crumbs from becoming mixed with the icing. Almond paste must not be overhandled during mixing or it will become oily and spoil the appearance of the icing. It freezes well (see page 10).

*Royal icing*, made with egg white and icing (confectioner's) sugar, is applied over almond paste to rich fruit cakes for Christmas, weddings, christenings and other special occasions. As it is very firm, it will hold decorations well and may be used for intricate piping. It is not suitable for light-textured cakes.

*Fondant icing* is a boiled icing based on a sugar syrup. It can be rolled out and used to coat light cakes or fruit cakes; it is usually applied over a coating of almond paste. Fondant icing can also be moulded into flowers and other shapes for cake decoration, but is not suitable for piping. As it keeps well in a refrigerator, it is worth making a good quantity at one time.

*Uncooked fondant icing* is very easy to make and can be rolled out to coat cakes, and moulded to make decorative shapes.

It can also be bought ready made, and merely rolled out and shaped as liked.

*American frosting* is another boiled icing which needs a sugar thermometer for success. It sets firmly but has a soft texture and may be used on sponges and layered cakes. It may be used instead of royal icing for fruit cakes without almond paste underneath. It must be handled quickly, as it sets fast; it is not suitable for piping. American frosting keeps well.

# GLACÉ ICING

*To ice top of 20cm/8 inch cake*

| Metric/imperial | | American |
|---|---|---|
| 225g/8 oz | icing (confectioner's) sugar, sifted | 2 cups |
| 1–2 × 15ml spoons/1–2 tablespoons | cold water | 1–3 tablespoons |
| | food colouring (optional) | |

Place the icing (confectioner's) sugar in a mixing bowl, and mix smoothly with 1 × 15ml spoon/1 tablespoon cold water for a firm consistency, or 2 × 15ml spoons/2 tablespoons/3 US tablespoons for a soft flowing consistency.

To give an extra shine to glacé icing, dissolve the icing sugar and water by stirring in a saucepan over gentle heat.

Beat the icing well. Colouring may be added at this stage: use a fine skewer to add it drop by drop.

Pour the icing on to the cake. Spread quickly with a palette knife (metal spatula), using long sweeping movements.

To add decorations, dip them in a little glacé icing, and arrange on the cake when half-set. Leave to set completely.

**Note**  Use 175g/6 oz/1½ US cups sugar for a 17.5cm/7 inch cake and 350g/12 oz/3 US cups sugar for a 25cm/10 inch cake. If a cake is more than 5cm/2 inches deep, double the quantities to coat the top and sides.

## Variations
**Chocolate Glacé Icing**
Substitute 2 × 5ml spoons/2 teaspoons/3 US teaspoons cocoa powder dissolved in 1 × 15ml spoon/1 tablespoon hot water for the cold water.
**Coffee Glacé Icing**
Substitute coffee essence (strong black coffee) for water.
**Orange Glacé Icing**
Use fresh orange juice instead of water.
**Lemon Glacé Icing**
Use fresh lemon juice instead of water.

# BUTTERCREAM

*To coat top of 20cm/8 inch cake*

| Metric/imperial | | American |
|---|---|---|
| 100g/4 oz | unsalted butter, softened | 1 stick |
| 225g/8 oz | icing (confectioner's) sugar, sifted | 2 cups |
| 1 × 5ml spoon/ 1 teaspoon | hot water | 1 teaspoon |
| | vanilla flavouring | |

Put the butter in a mixing bowl, and beat until creamy. Gradually add the sugar, and beat with a wooden spoon until light and fluffy. Beat in the water and vanilla flavouring to taste.

Put the buttercream on top of the cake, and spread out in long sweeping movements with a palette knife (metal spatula), or swirl with the back of a spoon. Leave to set.

**Note**  Use 75g/3 oz/6 US tablespoons butter for a 17.5cm/ 7 inch cake, or 175g/6 oz/1½ US sticks butter for a 25cm/10 inch cake, varying the other ingredients in proportion. Use double quantities for coating the top and filling one layer, and treble quantities for the top, filling and sides.

## Variations

**Chocolate Buttercream**
Add 40g/1½ oz/¼ US cups melted chocolate, and omit the hot water and vanilla flavouring.

**Coffee Buttercream**
Substitute coffee essence (strong black coffee) for the water, and omit the vanilla flavouring.

**Orange Buttercream**
Substitute fresh orange juice for the water and add 1 × 5ml spoon/1 teaspoon finely grated orange rind. Omit the vanilla flavouring.

**Lemon Buttercream**
Substitute fresh lemon juice for the water and add 1 × 5ml spoon/1 teaspoon finely grated lemon rind. Omit the vanilla flavouring.

# ALMOND PASTE

*To coat the top of 20cm/8 inch cake*

| Metric/imperial | | American |
|---|---|---|
| 100g/4 oz | icing (confectioner's) sugar, sifted | 1 cup |
| 100g/4 oz | caster (fine) sugar | ½ cup |
| 225g/8 oz | ground almonds | 2 cups |
| 1 × 5ml spoon/ 1 teaspoon | lemon juice | 1 teaspoon |
| | a few drops almond flavouring | |
| | 1 egg, beaten | |
| 2 × 15ml spoons/ 2 tablespoons | apricot jam, warmed and sieved | 3 tablespoons |

Combine the sugars in a mixing bowl and add the almonds, lemon juice and almond flavouring. Add enough egg to bind and give a firm paste.

Knead lightly until smooth on a board sprinkled with icing (confectioner's) sugar—do not overhandle. Roll out on a lightly floured surface, and cut out a 20cm/8 inch circle.

Brush the top of the cake with the jam. Cover with the almond paste, and press down firmly. Leave, uncovered, for 48 hours to dry out before icing.

**Note**  Use 175g/6 oz/1½ US cups ground almonds for the top of a 22.5cm/9 inch round cake and 225g/8 oz/2 US cups almonds for the top of a 25cm/10 inch round cake. Double the quantities if you wish to coat the sides of the cake as well.

# Rich Almond Paste

*To coat the top and sides of 25cm/10 inch cake*

| Metric/imperial | | American |
|---|---|---|
| 450g/1 lb | ground almonds | 4 cups |
| 450g/1 lb | icing (confectioner's) sugar, sifted | 4 cups |
| 1 × 5ml spoon/ 1 teaspoon | vanilla flavouring | 1 teaspoon |
| 1 × 5ml spoon/ 1 teaspoon | brandy | 1 teaspoon |
| | juice of 1 lemon | |
| 1 × 2.5ml spoon/ ½ teaspoon | orange flower water | ½ teaspoon |
| | 2 eggs, beaten | |

Combine the ground almonds and icing (confectioner's) sugar in a mixing bowl. Add the remaining ingredients, and work together to make a stiff paste.

Knead lightly on a board sprinkled with icing (confectioner's) sugar until the paste is smooth and glossy.

To coat the cake, proceed as for Almond Paste (see page 74).

# Royal Icing

*To coat and pipe top and sides of 17.5cm/7 inch round cake*

| Metric/imperial | | American |
|---|---|---|
| | 2 egg whites | |
| 450g/1 lb | icing (confectioner's) sugar, sifted | 4 cups |
| 1 × 15ml spoon/ 1 tablespoon | lemon juice | 1 tablespoon |

In a mixing bowl, whisk the egg whites lightly until frothy. Very gradually beat in the icing (confectioner's) sugar. Add the lemon juice, and continue beating until the icing forms soft peaks and is very white.

Reserve a little of the icing for piping, and put the remainder on top of the cake coated with almond paste. Using a palette knife (metal spatula), gradually work the icing out from the centre over the top and down the sides. Spread evenly over the sides of the cake. Neaten the top by drawing a straight-edged knife or ruler across the surface. Neaten the sides with vertical movements of the knife or ruler. Leave to set.

Beat the reserved icing until it forms stiff peaks, then place in a piping bag and use to pipe the top of the cake decoratively. Leave to set.

**Note** If the icing is made before it is needed, cover the bowl with a damp cloth to prevent it from hardening.

If a softer icing is preferred, add 1 × 5ml spoon/1 teaspoon glycerine to the mixture.

Special occasion cakes should have two thinner coats of Royal Icing, rather than one thick one, and the first coat must be allowed to dry thoroughly before the second is applied. Double the quantities for two coats.

# FONDANT ICING

*To coat top and sides of 20cm/8 inch round cake*

| Metric/imperial | | American |
|---|---|---|
| 150ml/¼ pint | water | ⅝ cup |
| 450g/1 lb | sugar | 2 cups |
| | a large pinch of cream of tartar | |
| | food flavouring and colouring | |

Place the water and sugar in a large heavy-based saucepan, and heat gently, without stirring, until the sugar is dissolved. Bring to the boil, add the cream of tartar, and boil to 120°C/240°F. Add flavouring and colouring to taste, then pour into a bowl, and leave to cool until a skin forms on top.

Beat the icing until it thickens, then turn on to a cold surface and work with a round-bladed knife until thick and smooth. Knead to a thick, creamy consistency.

Place the icing in a bowl set over a saucepan of gently simmering water, then heat until the consistency of thick cream.

Pour on to an almond paste-coated cake, or dip small cakes into the icing. Leave to set.

# UNCOOKED FONDANT ICING

*To coat top and sides of 20cm/8 inch round cake*

| Metric/imperial | | American |
|---|---|---|
| 4 × 15ml spoons/ 4 tablespoons | liquid glucose | 5 tablespoons |
| 450g/1 lb | icing (confectioner's) sugar, sifted | 4 cups |
| | 1 egg white | |
| | food flavouring and colouring | |

Place the glucose in a cup, and stand in a pan of hot water to soften. Place the icing (confectioner's) sugar in a mixing bowl, add the glucose and egg white, and beat to make a stiff paste. Add flavouring and colouring to taste, and beat again.

Turn on to a board sprinkled with icing (confectioner's) sugar, and knead well until smooth. Roll out on a board sprinkled with cornflour (cornstarch), to a circle large enough to cover the top of the cake and come half-way down the sides.

Place the icing on the cake, and mould down the sides. Leave to set.

*Fondant Icing* **and** *Almond Paste (page 74) are used to make Iced Fancies (page 50)*

# AMERICAN FROSTING

*To fill and coat 20cm/8 inch round cake*

| Metric/imperial | | American |
|---|---|---|
| 225g/8 oz | sugar | 1 cup |
| 4 × 15ml spoons/ 4 tablespoons | water | 5 tablespoons |
| | 1 egg white | |
| | food flavouring and colouring | |

Place the sugar and water in a heavy-based saucepan, and heat gently, stirring, until the sugar is dissolved. Heat to 120°C/240°F without further stirring.

In a large mixing bowl, beat the egg white until it forms stiff peaks. Remove the sugar syrup from the heat, and, when the bubbles subside, gradually whisk it into the egg white, with food flavouring and colouring to taste, until the mixture thickens and becomes opaque.

Pour the frosting quickly on to the cake, swirling it into peaks with a palette knife (metal spatula). Leave until set.

# SEVEN-MINUTE FROSTING

*To fill and coat 20cm/8 inch round cake*

| Metric/imperial | | American |
|---|---|---|
| | 1 egg white | |
| 175g/6 oz | sugar | scant 1 cup |
| 2 × 15ml spoons/ 2 tablespoons | cold water | 3 tablespoons |
| ½ × 2.5ml spoon/ ¼ teaspoon | cream of tartar | ¼ teaspoon |
| | a pinch of salt | |

Place all the ingredients in the top of a double saucepan, or in a bowl set over a saucepan of hot water. Bring the water to the boil, and whisk the sugar mixture vigorously for 7 minutes until it forms stiff peaks. Scrape the sides of the pan or bowl from time to time with a spatula.

Pour the frosting over the cake, and swirl into peaks with a palette knife (metal spatula). Leave until set.

# HONEY FROSTING

*To fill and coat 20cm/8 inch round cake*

| Metric/imperial | | American |
|---|---|---|
| 175g/6 oz | clear honey | ½ cup |
| | 1 egg white | |

Place the honey in a heavy-based saucepan, and heat to 120°C/240°F. In a mixing bowl, whisk the egg white until it forms stiff peaks. Beat in the hot honey, and continue beating until the mixture is thick enough to hold its shape.

Swirl the frosting over the cake, and leave to cool and set.

**Note**   This frosting is delicious on spice cakes and gingerbread.

# COCONUT FROSTING

*To fill and coat 20cm/8 inch round cake*

| Metric/imperial | | American |
|---|---|---|
| 175g/6 oz | soft dark brown sugar | 1 cup, packed |
| 50g/2 oz | desiccated (shredded) coconut | ¾ cup, loosely packed |
| 2 × 15ml spoons/ 2 tablespoons | melted butter | 3 tablespoons |
| 3 × 15ml spoons/ 3 tablespoons | double (heavy) cream | 4 tablespoons |

Blend together all the ingredients in a mixing bowl, and beat until thoroughly combined. Spread on top of the warm cake. Place under a medium-hot grill (broiler) until golden-brown. Leave to cool and set.

**Note** This frosting should be made while the cake is baking. It is particularly good on plain cakes.

# COFFEE FUDGE FROSTING

*To fill and coat 20cm/8 inch round cake*

| Metric/imperial | | American |
|---|---|---|
| 50g/2 oz | unsalted butter | 4 tablespoons |
| 350g/12 oz | icing (confectioner's) sugar, sifted | 3 cups |
| 2 × 15ml spoons/ 2 tablespoons | coffee essence (strong black coffee) | 3 tablespoons |
| 2 × 15ml spoons/ 2 tablespoons | single (light) cream | 3 tablespoons |

Place the butter in a saucepan, and heat very gently until melted. Remove from the heat and beat in half the icing (confectioner's) sugar and the coffee essence. Beat in the remaining sugar until smooth, then beat in the cream to give a spreading consistency.

Swirl the frosting over the top of the cake, and leave to cool and set.

# INDEX OF RECIPES